W. Armitstead

A GOODLY FELLOWSHIP

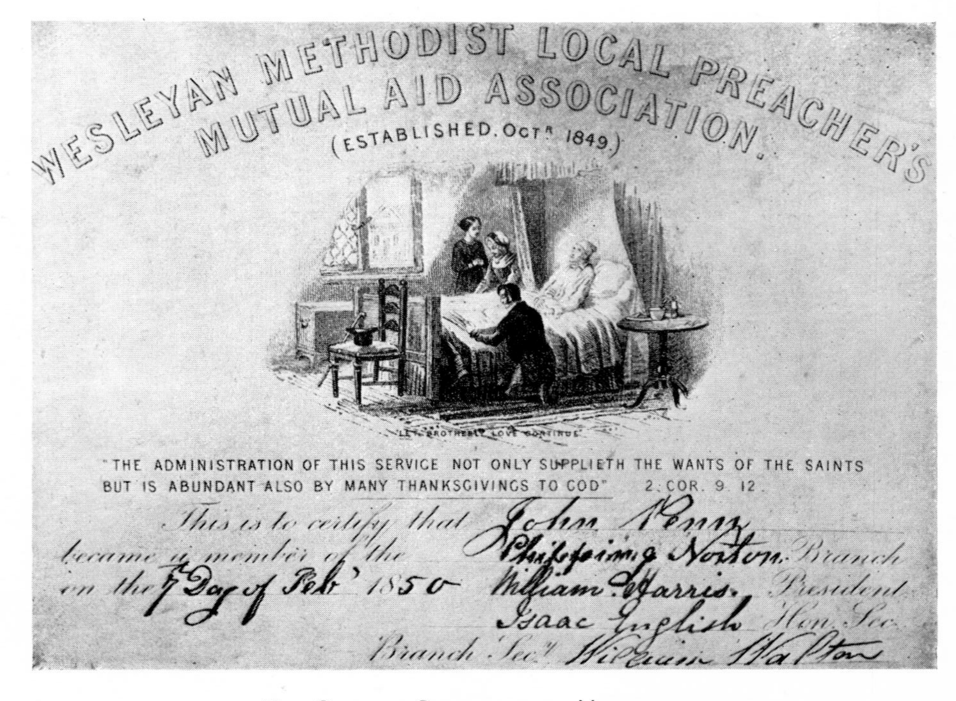

WESLEYAN METHODIST LOCAL PREACHER'S
MUTUAL AID ASSOCIATION.
(ESTABLISHED. OCTR 1849.)

"LET BROTHERLY LOVE CONTINUE"

"THE ADMINISTRATION OF THIS SERVICE NOT ONLY SUPPLIETH THE WANTS OF THE SAINTS BUT IS ABUNDANT ALSO BY MANY THANKSGIVINGS TO GOD" 2. COR. 9. 12.

This is to certify that John [illegible]
became a member of the Chipping Norton Branch
on the 7th Day of Feb. 1850 William Harris President
Isaac English Hon. Sec.
Branch Secy. William Walton

The Original Certificate of Membership

A GOODLY FELLOWSHIP

A History of the Hundred Years of the Methodist Local Preachers Mutual Aid Association: 1849–1949

by

F. HAROLD BUSS

and

R. G. BURNETT

LONDON: THE EPWORTH PRESS

Published by
THE EPWORTH PRESS
(FRANK H. CUMBERS)
25-35 City Road, London, E.C.1

*

New York - *Toronto*
Melbourne - *Cape Town*

First published in 1949.

PRINTED AND BOUND IN ENGLAND BY
HAZELL WATSON & VINEY LTD
AYLESBURY AND LONDON

The fellowship in the ministering to the saints.

2 CORINTHIANS 8 [4].

Fellowship is life, and lack of fellowship is death: and the deeds that ye do upon the earth, it is for fellowship's sake that ye do them, and the life that is in it, that shall live on and on for ever.

—WILLIAM MORRIS: *A Dream of John Ball.*

FOREWORD

THIS BOOK is the product of a happy partnership rather than of a collaboration in the usual sense of that word. The two Parts have been written independently, and each of the joint authors is responsible for his own section only. The shape and substance of the book have been the subject of constant conference between them, and they count it a privilege to have been associated in this labour of love in behalf of the Association they both delight to serve.

This record of the Association's hundred years of service and ministering to the poor and needy is sent forth in the prayerful hope that it may furnish an acceptable memorial of a great and Christlike institution, whose work has from the beginning been inspired and blessed by the Father of mercies and the Lord of love.

F. H. B.
R. G. B.

CONTENTS

PART ONE

The Story of the Mutual Aid Association: 1849 to 1949

PART TWO

The *Local Preachers' Magazine* and Character Sketches of Mutual Aid Leaders

ILLUSTRATIONS

PART ONE

The Story of the Mutual Aid Association 1849-1949

William Harris

First President of the Association

CHAPTER ONE

HOW IT ALL BEGAN

THE YEAR 1849 was for Methodism a year of ferment and conflict and unhappy division. Rumblings of the coming storm had for a long time disturbed the peace and fellowship of the Church. Discontent with the arbitrary and rigid rule of the authorities in Conference was steadily growing, and in 1845 the first of the four notorious *Fly Sheets* was published, the last of these appearing in 1848. Rancorous and intemperate in tone and language, these anonymous squibs were devoted less to reasoned argument for reform than to reckless abuse of the ruling powers. Among these powers, the dominating and domineering figure of Dr. Jabez Bunting stood out above the rest, and it was upon his imperious ascendancy that the agitation was chiefly focused. 'The actual government of Methodism at this period', says Dr. Benjamin Gregory, 'was an autocracy, strengthened by an oligarchy.' Obviously, this dictatorship of the few could not endure. Liberal ideas were abroad in the body politic, and must in time have sapped the foundation of the fortress of clerical arrogance. It reveals, therefore, a lamentable lack of wisdom and grace that the reformers should have chosen to indulge in scurrilous and defamatory personalities, rather than by patient and orderly discussion to urge their case against ecclesiastical obscurantism.

The immediate effect of these vituperative sheets was to inspire attempts to answer them in kind, and five

Papers on Wesleyan Matters were issued, also anonymously. Inasmuch as these defenders of hierarchical authority were as unscrupulous and insulting as their opponents, they did more harm than good, and served only to embitter and intensify the controversy. In the Conference of 1849, held in Manchester, the long-gathering storm broke, and Methodism suffered a grievous hurt. An unedifying debate ended in three ministers being expelled. As the reputed champions of liberty and progress against illiberal and intolerant Conference potentates, their case evoked much sympathy in the religious Press and in religious circles, and many Methodists followed the banished ministers into exile. Two years later the Conference had to report a decrease of more than 56,000 members, the majority of whom had probably thrown in their lot with the dissidents.

This is not the place to discuss the rights and wrongs of these 'old, unhappy, far-off things, and battles' of a hundred years ago. This book is not a history of Methodism, but the story of a work of love and charity that was begun in Methodism's darkest hour: 'this distressing year of Methodism', Dr. George Smith calls it, 'a season of deep affliction to all spiritually-minded men, a day of gloominess and of thick darkness'. It was in the year when the clouds were thickest and most threatening over their beloved Church that a little company of local preachers turned their thoughts to the needs of their afflicted and aged brethren, and the Mutual Aid Association was born. Dr. Smith describes the proceedings of 1849 as 'that memorable epoch in Wesleyan history'. Neither he nor even that band of brothers knew how memorable the date was to be. 'Tall oaks from little acorns grow', but who could have foreseen that the tiny seed planted by a few devoted and kindly men, while the fierce winds and waves of controversy were rocking the Church, would grow into a mighty tree whose leaves have been for the healing, succour, and shelter of countless numbers of afflicted and needy servants of God?

The conditions of penury and privation in which many local preachers were living had for some years been causing grave concern to their brethren. It was felt as a bitter disappointment when the Wesleyan Conference refused to allocate a part of the Centenary Fund of 1839 to relieve the distress of these 'Helpers', as John Wesley called his lay preachers. The Fund amounted in all to nearly £300,000. More than half of this sum was divided between the Theological Institution and the Missionary Society, and over £16,000 was given to the Worn-out Ministers' and Widows' Relief Fund. Not a penny was offered by Conference for the assistance of the necessitous lay apostles and evangelists of the Church. James Wild, who became the Mutual Aid Association's first Treasurer, had proposed the setting up of a fund for that purpose, and had promised to give £100 toward it, but the project met with no response from ministerial officialdom. It became increasingly evident that, if anything was to be done, the brethren would have to do it themselves.

The insurgent section of the Methodist society had not been slow to promulgate their opinions through the medium of the Press, and a variety of journals made a brief appearance and a swift departure. One of these papers which enjoyed a longer life than most was the *Wesleyan Times*. Its first number came out on 8th January 1849. Three weeks later, in its issue of 30th January, appeared a report of a meeting of the 'Bristol Local Preachers Mutual Aid Association' which was formed, as was stated by the president, John Russom, 'for the purpose of promoting brotherly love, relieving the distressed, administering to the wants and necessities of the afflicted, and smoothing the pillow of death'. An editorial comment in the paper runs: 'The local preachers of the City of Bristol have taken the lead in this important matter, and while we wish them success, we hope that their example will be speedily followed in every circuit in the Connexion. We would rather not have a number of local institutions like that in Bristol, but one large Society, embracing all the preachers in the Connexion; and we see no great difficulty in the way of the formation of such an Association. Its benefits would be incalculable.'[1]

The Bristol brethren must be given due credit for their pioneer service in associating together for mutual aid, but theirs was not the only society formed for such a purpose. One had been established in Cambridge in 1846, and there were others. These were all limited to their own localities, and nothing seems to have been done to extend and co-ordinate the good work throughout the Connexion.

Then one evening, in a cottage in Matlock village, which was then in the Cromford Wesleyan circuit,[2] two Wesleyan local preachers sat talking. One had been musing on the blessing that might spring from a meeting together of brethren for intercourse and fellowship, and he mentioned his idea to his friend. 'Oh, what a happy thought,' responded the other; 'if such a meeting could be gathered together, we might endeavour to form

[1] Quoted from *A Brief Account of the Wesleyan Methodist Local Preachers Mutual Aid Association*, by A. Russell Johnson, 1885.

[2] In this circuit, Elizabeth Evans, the original of 'Dinah Morris' in George Eliot's *Adam Bede*, and her husband, Samuel Evans ('Seth Bede'), were living at this time. S. Evans appears on the Plan as an accredited local preacher. Preaching by women was frowned on by Conference, but 'Dinah's' gifts, grace, and fruits could not be denied. Cromford was one of the places where she frequently preached. She died on 9th November 1849, the year in which the Mutual Aid Association was born, and a memorial tablet is placed in the Wirksworth Ebenezer Wesleyan Chapel.

a society for the benefit of the sick and poor among the local preachers of Methodism.' This was the account given by Francis Pearson, when speaking in the public meeting at Birmingham in 1850. He did not mention the name of his companion, but a letter published in the *Local Preachers' Magazine* in 1889 reveals his identity as Joseph H. Marsden, and the date of this fateful conversation as 21st May 1849. Owing to ill health, Marsden was not able to take an active part in the organization of the new movement, but he did what he could with his pen.

He died in Sheffield in 1885, assisted in his latter years by the Association whose existence his words had done so much to inspire.

Deeply impressed by this suggestion of a benevolent society for the relief of his afflicted and aged brethren, Pearson was moved to compose a letter urging that a gathering of local preachers should be summoned to take counsel together on this problem in particular, and on other matters connected with their calling. This letter he sent for publication in the *Watchman* and the *Wesleyan Times*. The former paper had been founded in January 1835 as an organ of news and views in support of the constituted authorities of Methodism. As its prospectus declared, it was 'pledged to uphold and defend, as occasion may require, the principles and economy of Wesleyan Methodism, as settled by its venerable Founder, and by the Conference since his decease'. It is perhaps not surprising that a journal so stoutly loyalist should decline to print Pearson's letter. Ten years before, the Centenary Fund Committee had excluded indigent local preachers from benefiting from the bounteous giving of the Methodist people, and the same lack of feeling and imagination still prevailed in official quarters. Who could tell what perilous stuff lurked within the innocent-seeming proposal? Who knew what mischief was afoot among the conspiring laymen? So suspicion and ignorance combined to ban the offending, and possibly dangerous, epistle from the *Watchman's* virtuous pages.

To its lasting credit, the *Wesleyan Times* displayed a more discerning understanding of the conditions which gave rise to the suggestion, and obligingly printed Pearson's letter. Much correspondence ensued in the columns of the newspaper, and more than two hundred letters were received by Pearson himself, approving or inquiring about the scheme. Encouraged by this response, he wrote a second letter, which appeared in the *Wesleyan Times* on 19th June. This time he formulated a specific object for the proposed meeting to achieve, namely, 'the formation of a Society composed of local preachers *only*, for the purpose of affording pecuniary relief to the sick and necessitous amongst us'.

The interest already kindled was, by this proposal, fanned into a flame, and meetings of brethren were held in all parts of the country to consider how support might be given to this bold and novel enterprise. Enheartened by these manifestations, Pearson felt that the time was ripe for taking a definite and practical step toward the end in view, and invitations were issued for a preparatory meeting in Birmingham.

Prior to that meeting, the following circular was sent to all the local preachers in London.

LONDON, *July* 16, 1849.

DEAR BROTHER,

We respectfully invite your attendance at a Meeting of the Wesleyan Methodist Local Preachers of the London Circuits, on Wednesday next, July 18th, at Seven o'clock in the evening, at Hart's Temperance Hotel, Aldersgate Street, City, to consider the desirability and practicability of the proposed 'General Benevolent

Fund for Local Preachers', and the propriety of holding an Aggregate Meeting in furtherance of that object.

Hoping that nothing will prevent your being present,

We are, dear Brother, yours in Christian bonds,

E. CRESWELL, 5 Albert Terrace, Knightsbridge.
W. BOWRON, 43 Grosvenor Row, Pimlico.
W. HARRIS, 4 Barnsbury Place, Islington.
W. NASH, Ball's Pond.

Upward of seventy brethren attended this meeting in Aldersgate Street (a name great and famous in Methodist story), cordially approved the formation of a society for the assistance of local preachers in sickness, distress, and old age, and elected Isaac English and William Harris as delegates to the Birmingham meeting.

The momentous synod was held on Tuesday 24th July. Twenty-four brethren were present, and the names of most of them are on record: J. Russom (Bristol), J. U. Walker (Halifax), J. Flatman (Downham), J. Morgan (Hanley), Rowland (Ripley), Horton (Wednesbury), Sharman, Collier, Howarth (Sheffield), F. Pearson, G. Marriott, J. Hodgkinson (Matlock), Hodgkinson (Derby), I. English, W. Harris (London), E. Cope, A. Brooks, H. Smith, W. Page, and J. Butcher (Birmingham). Francis Pearson outlined his plan, and after a day of prayerful and careful discussion, certain resolutions were adopted. The minute ran as follows:

A meeting of local preachers from various parts of the Kingdom was held in Birmingham on Tuesday, July 24, 1849, for the purpose of considering the best means to be adopted for the formation of a Fund for the Relief of Distressed Local Preachers in the Wesleyan Methodist Connexion.

The meeting having opened with prayer, Brother William Harris, of London, was unanimously voted to the chair, and Brother A. Brooks, of Birmingham, to the Secretaryship, when the following resolutions were passed unanimously:

1. That this meeting form itself into a Committee, with power to add to its number, for the purpose of considering the best means of providing relief for distressed Local Preachers in the Wesleyan Methodist Connexion.

2. That this meeting recommends that a Society be now formed, to be called—The General Wesleyan Methodist Local Preachers Mutual Aid Association.

3. That the object contemplated by this meeting shall be to afford assistance to local preachers in times of sickness, distress, and old age.

4. That the entrance fee into this Society be 10/-.

5. That the terms of subscription be 2*d.* per week.

6. That all persons contributing One Guinea per annum become Honorary Members.

7. That this meeting is strongly of opinion that the rules of the Society be formed upon principles giving the claimants upon the Fund a right to relief and recommends this resolution to the serious consideration of a future meeting.

8. That the Officers of the Association shall consist of President, Vice-Presidents, Treasurer, Secretaries, and Committees.

9. That the cordial thanks of this meeting be presented to Brother F. Pearson for his very efficient services in promoting hitherto the object of this Association, and that he be respectfully requested to be the Corresponding Secretary for the further carrying out of its measures.

10. That the following brethen be appointed District Secretaries:

Mr. J. U. Walker (Halifax) Mr. A. Brooks (Birmingham)
Mr. J. Russom (Bristol) Mr. J. Flatman (Norfolk)
Mr. E. Creswell (London) Mr. J. Morgan (Burslem)

And that they be requested to communicate with friends in various Districts.

11. That an Aggregate Meeting be held in London on the 3rd and 4th October next, and that each Circuit be requested to send a Representative, in addition to those who may voluntarily attend.

On their return from Birmingham, English and Harris gave the London Committee a report of the proceedings and resolutions, and the work of preparation for the inaugural gathering in October began in real earnest. Information and invitations were issued to the brethren in the country circuits, and representatives of the eight London circuits met to arrange hospitality and accommodation for the visiting delegates. The work was complicated by a violent epidemic of cholera which affected London and the whole Kingdom, more than

50,000 persons dying of the disease in England and Wales in 1848-9. Many people left London for fear of the plague, and many intending visitors discreetly decided to remain at a safe distance. But in spite of all discouragements, the planners went on with their planning, and as always has been the case in connection with the Association's gatherings, the opportunities for spiritual fellowship and inspiration presented by such an assembling together of brethren were not neglected. A preaching service in Great Queen Street Chapel and a Communion service in City Road Chapel were arranged with the approval of the Rev. Thomas Jackson, President of the Conference, and the Revs. J. Lomas and Israel Holgate, Superintendents of the Circuits. One of the first acts of the new General Committee was to express their thanks to these ministers for their kindness and assistance in furthering the arrangements for these religious services. The sessions for business were to be held in the Freemasons' Hall, in Great Queen Street. On Tuesday 2nd October the members of the London Committee were joined by the brethren who had met in Birmingham. With hymns and prayers, and in the utmost harmony and concord, the day was spent in discussing the Birmingham resolutions, and reshaping them for presentation to the great meeting on the morrow.

All things were now ready. The pioneers had done their work well. The way was prepared and made straight for their brethren to go in and possess the land. It was to prove 'a good land'; 'a land of brooks of water, of fountains and depths; a land of bread without scarceness; thou shalt not lack anything in it; a land which the Lord thy God careth for'.

CHAPTER TWO

THE FOUNDATIONS ARE LAID

THE FOLLOWING advertisement, which appeared in both the *Watchman* and the *Wesleyan Times*, was the first announcement to the Methodist public of the new adventure astir in their midst.

GENERAL WESLEYAN METHODIST LOCAL PREACHERS MUTUAL AID ASSOCIATION.—The Aggregate Meeting will be held on Wednesday and Thursday next, the 3rd and 4th of October, 1849, in Freemasons' Hall, Great Queen Street, Lincoln's Inn Fields, to commence each day at nine a.m. precisely. Public Religious Services—Dr. Melson, of Birmingham, has consented to preach the Sermon to the Brethren, at Great Queen Street Chapel, on Wednesday evening next. Service to commence at seven o'clock. —On Thursday evening, the Sacrament of the Lord's Supper will be administered to the Brethren, in City Road Chapel, by the Ministers of the Circuit. Service to commence at seven o'clock.— It is hoped that all the Local Preachers belonging to the Circuits in and around London will, if possible, attend the meetings, and give their country brethren a hearty and cordial reception. The brethren will be expected to bring their Circuit Plans and Society Tickets with them.

By order of the Committee,
EDWARD CRESWELL,
Hon. Secretary.

5 Albert Terrace,
Knightsbridge.
September 29, 1849.

Probably few people, other than local preachers, read it at all, and fewer still attached any importance to it. Even the most enthusiastic promoters of the movement could have had no idea of the greatness to which this thing would grow; still less would they, or any Methodist alive, have believed that it would become one of the best beloved institutions in Methodism. Suspicion, misrepresentation, and opposition were encountered from the beginning, but though the brethren were reviled they reviled not again, and in an address 'To the Wesleyan Methodist Local Preachers of Great Britain' the Committee urged them to maintain a spirit of charitableness toward their critics, to exercise patience, and to let no word or action cause their good to be evil spoken of. They felt conscious that God would approve their work, for it was in obedience to Him that they were attempting to do good to those who were 'of the household of faith'. Never is there any sign of self-seeking among the earliest members of this confraternity of preachers of the Gospel, nor do they allow the noise of the 'hostile feuds' raging around them to disturb their peaceful pursuance of the end in view.

So at last the great day dawned, the day hoped for, prayed for, worked for, the day which saw 'the First Aggregate Meeting of Local Preachers for the Formation of a Mutual Aid Association'. A note may be appropriate here about the use of the term 'Aggregate'. In later years suggestions have been made that the somewhat uncouth word might give place to a simpler and more attractive title, but nothing more accurate and suitable has been found. The word means literally 'to bring into the flock' and what could be more expressive of the coming together of those who are of one heart and mind? Geologically, an 'aggregate' is composed of different minerals, combined into one rock, which again is not a bad picture of the uniting love which binds into one firm brotherhood those whose hearts are fired with a common enthusiasm. It is not likely that a term which is hallowed by age, and by so many happy and precious memories, will be surrendered now.

It was in keeping with the sacred nature of their task

that the brethren should begin the day with a prayer-meeting. This was held at seven o'clock in the morning in Great Queen Street Chapel. Perhaps men were 'made of sterner stuff' a hundred years ago, for this good custom has long since passed into desuetude. Nearly seven hundred brethren were present when the Aggregate Meeting opened with Charles Wesley's hymn:

Behold, how good a thing
It is to dwell in peace;
How pleasing to our King
This fruit of righteousness;
When brethren all in one agree,
Who knows the joys of unity!

This hymn fell under the axe of the revisers responsible for the 1933 collection; we could have better spared other hymns that were included. William Harris, of Islington, who was chairman of the London Committee, was elected with acclamation to preside over the great Meeting. He accepted the call, with the modest deprecation, customary with all persons raised to such positions of eminence, that he had not sought it and was undeserving of it, and then proceeded to deliver a lengthy address which reads as if he was not surprised by the honour. He explained the objects of the gathering, and emphasized the duty of the Church to care for the poor, illustrating the peculiar and pressing need of many local preachers by recounting a story which had been told at the Birmingham meeting by James Uriah Walker, of Halifax. The story is worthy of record as an example of the pitiable conditions which moved the founders of the Association to enter upon their compassionate ministry:

A few years since, I was Poor Law guardian. The first man whom I ever remember hearing preach the Gospel was a poor local preacher. The sound of his voice is associated with my earliest impressions, and is continually, from such early remembrances, ringing in my ears. I sat at the Board one day, and who should come in to ask for relief but this brother? I felt ashamed when he came in. By my side sat a brother guardian, who was a Churchman, and I saw him, as I hung my head with something like confusion, quickening his gaze and looking with more attentiveness than usual. As the brother came to the table he said to me: 'Is not this one of your people?' The inquiry deepened my confusion, but I was obliged to say: 'Yes, he is.' He made a second inquiry and said: 'Is he not one of your preachers?' The truth escaped from me a second time, and I replied affirmatively. 'Sir,' said the Churchman, tapping me on the elbow, 'this ought not to be. This brother of yours, this Methodist preacher, ought not to have come to this Poor Law Board for relief,' and thrusting his hand into his pocket, he said: 'I will give something to relieve him, if you will do so, and we will not enter his name here.' From that day my mind was made up that some society ought to be formed for the relief of such cases.

After informing the meeting of the sympathy with their object expressed in many quarters, and the contributions and promises already received, the chairman besought the brethren not to introduce topics foreign to their purpose, and to shun everything that might impair their Christian temper and spirit. The meeting then turned to consideration of the Resolutions which had been agreed on by the preparatory united Committee. In view of the changes and developments of later years, it will be of interest to set forth here the propositions adopted when the Association's foundations first were laid.

RESOLUTIONS

1. That this Society be called the 'Wesleyan Methodist Local Preachers Mutual Aid Association'.

2. That this Association shall consist of accredited Local Preachers in Great Britain, and its object be to provide for relief in sickness, old age, and at death.

3. That there shall be no relief afforded, or other distribution of the funds of this Association, until the Association shall have been established for twelve calendar months.

4. That no Member shall be entitled to relief until he shall have been a Member and Subscriber for twelve calendar months.

5. That this Association shall be conducted by a General Committee, consisting of a President, Treasurer, Honorary Secretary,

and thirty Members, and that such officers shall be elected annually by the Aggregate Meeting.

6. That six or more Trustees shall be appointed; and in case of any vacancy, arising from death or any other cause, such vacancy to be filled up at the next annual meeting.

7. That every officer of this Institution shall be an accredited Local Preacher.

8. That the sum for admission to this Association be 10/-. That the subsequent subscription of each Member be 3/- per quarter, and the first quarter's subscription shall be payable on the first day of January, the first day of April, the first day of July, or the first day of October next after the entrance of such Member.

9. That the relief to be given by this Association in times of sickness shall not be less than 8/- per week.

10. That in case any Member of this Association shall cease to be a Local Preacher of the Wesleyan Methodist Society, from any cause whatever, but shall desire to continue a Member of this Association, it shall be lawful for the Local Brethren who are Members of this Association in the Circuit in which he resides, to inquire into the circumstances of the case, and in their discretion to declare that such person, although no longer a Local Preacher, shall still continue a Member of this Association, and be entitled to all the benefits of such membership, subject to the decision of the Annual Aggregate Meeting of the Association.

11. That if any Member of this Association shall be duly expelled from the Methodist Society for immorality, or shall, in the judgement of the Committee, be guilty of immorality, he shall also be expelled from this Association, and shall not, from thenceforth, be entitled to receive any benefit from the funds of the Association. Provided, nevertheless, that it shall be lawful for the General Committee, if they shall see fit, in cases of poverty or distress, to return the amount of money which shall have been paid by such Member, without interest, deducting therefrom any payments which shall have been made to such Member before such exclusion or retirement.

12. That all persons, not being Local Preachers, contributing One Guinea or upwards per annum be Honorary Members of this Association, and shall have the privilege of attending the Aggregate Meetings as spectators.

13. That so soon after the election of the Committee as they shall deem fit, in order to the proper management of the Association, they (the said Committee) shall be empowered to elect a paid Secretary, who shall find proper security, and shall be continued in office during their pleasure.

14. That whenever the amount of money in the hands of the Secretary, received by him for subscriptions, shall from time to time amount to the sum of £50, he shall pay the same into the hands of the Treasurer.

15. That when the amount in the hands of the Treasurer shall exceed the sum of £200 by the sum of £100, he shall invest such surplus amount in Government securities, in the names of the Trustees, who shall, at the request of the General Committee, from time to time sell out the same, or a sufficient part thereof, to be paid to the Treasurer for the purposes of this Association.

16. That the Committee forthwith be required to draw up Rules and Regulations for the government of this Association, embodying the foregoing resolutions; and as soon as these Rules are completed, communicate them to the Members of the General Body; such Rules to be subject to the approval of the next Aggregate Meeting.

17. That the Aggregate General Meeting shall have power, from time to time, to alter or to abrogate any of the Rules of this Association which have been, or may hereafter be, adopted.

18. That in order to sustain the deep affection and spiritual union reciprocated here these two days between the brethren, it is desirable that we hold a meeting of Local Preachers annually, and that our main object be the spiritual elevation and improvement of the brethren, to secure which arrangements be made for special religious services; and further, that the next meeting be held at Birmingham this time next year, and that the subsequent meetings be held in Whit-week.

19. That the next Aggregate Meeting be held for three days, and that the third day be entirely devoted to spiritual and religious services.

20. That in every case of appeal made to the General Meetings of this Association, by any Member thereof, such case shall be heard at a specified time, to be appointed by the Chairman, due information of which to be communicated to the individual appealing, and Local Preachers only to be present on such occasions.

It will be noted that these Resolutions are altered and amplified in many respects from those passed at Birmingham. The redundant word 'General' is dropped from the title; the annual subscription is fixed at 12*s*. instead of 8*s*. 8*d*.; only persons who are not local preachers can be honorary members; no member will be entitled to relief until twelve months after entrance; no mention is made of Vice-Presidents among the Executive officers. In addition, it is proposed that provision be made for devotional exercises and spiritual fellowship.

To Francis Pearson fell the honour of proposing the first resolution, and no man deserved it more. To him, more than to any other one person, this moment of opportunity was due. A writer in the first issue of the *Local Preachers' Magazine*, in January 1851, says of him: 'The labour, the anxiety, the perseverance, the expense, and above all, the disinterestedness which he has manifested from first to last in this affair is beyond all praise.' Pearson stressed the value of such an Association as a visible representation of the spiritual unity and brotherhood of local preachers throughout the land, and sounded an urgent call to prove their love of the brethren in more than word. He, too, had a moving instance of dire poverty to relate. John Turner was a local preacher in the Cromford circuit who lost his work, and then fell ill. It was 1846, and the failure of the harvest in England brought famine conditions to the very poor. For three months John had nothing to eat but the few cabbages and turnips his little garden grew. An honest and independent soul, he told no one of his straits. When his brethren did discover his conditions, and helped him as they could, he was too enfeebled for them to save him. A brother reported that he had found the sick man in bed, and in the house were his wife, and wife's mother, and a child, with only three-ha'p'orth of bread between them. Turner died soon after, and in accordance with his dying wish, Francis Pearson conducted the burial service. 'A man of God; we knew him, and loved him well; and for ability he would not have disgraced a London pulpit'; so his brother preacher spoke of John Turner. He starved to death on a diet of turnips and scanty crusts, while the Church which had just raised a quarter of a million pounds had nothing to spare to relieve the want of its lay preachers. It was told of another brother, 82 years of age and a preacher for sixty years, that his dinners for a week cost less than a shilling and often consisted only of a bit of herring. Others were in receipt of parish relief, and died and were buried as paupers. It is meet and necessary to recall these things for without an awareness of the poverty and insecurity and hardships of many of these unpaid messengers of God, we can never understand the urgency and passionate zeal with which their brethren determined to remedy these evil conditions. Some indeed would have gone further than the provisions in the second resolution. They wished to assist cases of distress due to unemployment and to make allowances to widows. But counsels of caution prevailed at this early stage, and it was deemed wiser not to proceed faster than the funds would allow. The third and fourth resolutions were approved without much divergence of opinion, James Wild, of Fulham, inspiring the brethren to find strength in union in their unquestionable right to go forward in the work they had in hand: 'Go, in the name of the Lord Jesus, to all who can help you, and tell them that it is time they did help you.' After tea, an informal experience meeting was held, and the brethren dispersed amid 'manifestations of brotherly love'.

Thursday's sessions began with another prayer meeting at seven o'clock in City Road Chapel, and then the delegates, to the number of between five hundred and six hundred, settled down to business again in Freemasons' Hall. The constitution of the General Committee was approved, after the suspicions of some provincial brethren with regard to the possible undue influence of London had been dispelled. 'I am a Yorkshire man, and in the habit of speaking out,' said a brother from

Tadcaster. On the question of the entrance fee and quarterly subscriptions, some difference of opinion was expressed, it being argued that 2*s*. per quarter and 5*s*. entrance fee would be as much as many could afford, but the original proposals were carried by a large majority. The amount of relief also caused some discussion, an amendment that it should be 10*s*. a week being made, but on a vote, this was not approved. It is worthy of note that the recognition of contributors of one guinea or upwards per annum as honorary members was not extended to local preachers. It was considered that it would introduce 'classification or caste', and it was insisted that, whatever a brother gave, he should stand on the same footing as those who paid only the usual entrance fee and quarterly subscription. The official resolutions having been duly confirmed, it now remained to elect the Association's first President. The obvious nomination of Francis Pearson was at once made, but on his firm refusal of the honour, the name of William Harris was proposed. Everyone rose to acclaim his election, and with expressions of befitting modesty, he accepted the responsibility. Resolutions 18 and 19 regarding the character and duration of future Aggregate Meetings were unanimously adopted, and the business terminated with the singing of the Doxology.

No report of the birthday of the Association would be complete without referring to the service on the Wednesday evening in Great Queen Street Chapel, conducted by Dr. Melson, a local preacher in the Birmingham West circuit. The Doctor preached to a crowded congregation from John 16, 8-11, and his sermon occupied an hour and forty-five minutes! A request that the discourse be printed as a commemoration of 'an era in Methodism' was heartily endorsed by the preacher's untired and intrepid hearers. The final official service

James Wild

President 1854; Hon. Treasurer 1849-1866

of this memorable occasion was held on Thursday evening in City Road Chapel, when the Sacrament of the Lord's Supper was adminstered by the circuit ministers, the Rev. Joseph Hargreaves delivering an address. And, to complete the record, mention should be made of the zeal of three brethren who, on the Friday, climbed into the gilded ball which surmounts the cupola of St. Paul's Cathedral, and sang a hymn, and held a prayer-meeting there.

So ended the historic days when the Association first began to be. Who would have dared to prophesy then its future growth and progress? 'Though thy beginning was small, yet thy latter end shall greatly increase.' Looking back, we can see that its architects and builders were inspired to build on sound foundations. The spiritual blessings of such a brotherhood were ever kept in view. They were preachers of the Word first, and then philanthropists. In all their doing they sought, as James Wild urged, 'to keep the fire of God alive in their own souls'. Though they were loyal to Methodism, they determined to keep free from Conference control, for they felt they could manage their own business better themselves. They resolutely refused to allow the conflicts in Methodism to be named among them, and banned all controversial questions in religion or politics, and above all, they kept steadily to their lofty aim of 'promoting brotherly love'. Their charitable work was the fruit of a fellowship of hearts. On these foundations these 'men of little showing' built well and truly, and the house of refuge they erected stands fair and firm to this day.

CHAPTER THREE

THE PROMISE OF A SHOWER

THE OFFICERS elected at the constitutive meeting of the Association on 4th October 1849 were:

President	*Treasurer*	*Secretary*
William Harris	James Wild	Edward Creswell

Trustees

Henry Reed (Scarborough)	Robert Swan Stanley (Newcastle)
Dr. Melson (Birmingham)	Richard Matthews (London)
Edward Brooke (Huddersfield)	Thomas Gurney (London)

Committee

Messrs. Pearson (Matlock-green), English (Deptford), Gandy (Spitalfields), Knight (Great Queen Street), Cope (Birmingham), Flatman (Downham), Walker (Halifax), Blake (Exeter), Hansom (London), Dabb (Southwark), Wood (London), Lovely (London), Volkman (Spitalfields), Jameson (Great Queen Street), Sharman (Sheffield), D. H. Harris (London), Keed (Lynn), Russom (Bristol), Curnock (Bristol), Smithson (York), Unwin (Sheffield), Nelstrop (Pontefract), Hurst (Ilkeston), Palmer (Belper), Crockford (Rochester), Davison (Sunderland), Towne (Melton Mowbray), Cluett (Wolverhampton), Bourne (City Road), Nichols (Great Queen Street), Johns (Newport).

These officials presented an account of their year's stewardship to the first Aggregate Meeting, properly so called, which was held in Birmingham on 2nd, 3rd, and 4th October 1850. An open meeting of the General Committee on Tuesday, the 1st, began with the historic hymn: 'And are we yet alive?', but the Aggregate Meeting started by singing the hymn used in the previous year: 'Behold, how good a thing.' Between two hundred and three hundred brethren were present when the President rose to review the first year's working.

He considered that the progress made was encouraging, and their 'little one' gave every promise of making 'a fine giant'. During the year, Edward Creswell had been appointed as the paid Secretary, and the first Annual Report was read by Isaac English, who had succeeded to the office of Honorary Secretary. The Report stated that, in order to save the expense of hiring offices, the Committee had met at first in the Treasurer's house, and then in each other's houses. The Rules had been drawn up and circulated, a card of membership had been designed, and account books for the use of Branches had been issued. The financial support received was gratifying, though more honorary members could have been desired. The membership was reported as 1,260, and the contributions amounted to £1,276 14*s.* 2*d.* On the whole, the Committee felt they had cause to congratulate the members that their plan to form such an Association, which was regarded by many as 'visionary', and viewed with suspicion and distrust, had succeeded so well; and they believed that, by the blessing of God, it would 'surmount every obstacle and form a bond of union and brotherhood hitherto unknown to the great body of Local Preachers in the Wesleyan Connexion'.

How gloriously the faith of our fathers was justified the history of the Association's hundred years abundantly declares.

The earliest Balance Sheet was but 'the promise of a shower', but the brethren saw and greeted the promise with joy. They believed that, if not in their day, then in His good time, God would prosper their faith's endeavour, and what was now a trickling rivulet would become a full and flowing river of blessing.

It was indeed 'a day of small things', but they were unwise who despised it. 'The little one shall become a thousand, and the small one a strong nation.' Here is the first financial statement:

DR.	£	s.	d.	CR.	£	s.	d.
Subscriptions and entrance fees ..	1276	14	2	Expenditure, as detailed at the meeting	196	18	8
Collections and Donations ..	59	18	0	Amounts in 3% Consols	1060	10	0
Sale of Reports, Rules, Cards, etc.	59	17	2	Balance in Treasurer's bank ..	138	0	8
	£1395	9	4		£1395	9	4

The printed Report of this first duly constituted Aggregate Meeting exhibits the brethren as possessed of a combination of vital piety and business acumen which all down the years has characterized the labourers in this cause. To increase the number of the General Committee to fifty members was a wise thing to do, but when the kindly sentiment of some would have raised the weekly allowance to ten shillings, and made orphans eligible for benefit, prudence counselled restraint. One brother wanted the word 'Conference' substituted for 'Aggregate Meeting'. He has had many successors since that primeval attempt, but none other name has found favour. As the then President pointed out: 'A Conference might mean only a few anywhere met together over a cup of tea, or in the chimney corner, and might even refer to old ladies met for friendly gossip; whereas an Aggregate Meeting suggested large numbers.' At this meeting it was proposed that, in connection with future Aggregate Meetings, a list of the religious services to be held should be drawn up, and also the names and addresses of the delegates given. This was carried by acclamation, after the President had enheartened the fearful souls, who saw difficulties in the way of obtaining pulpits, by reminding them of the ministerial help given them last year in London, and by paying a tribute to the courteous desire to assist shown by the present President of the Conference, Dr. Beecham. Again it was made manifest that the brethren were not content to come together to feed the hungry, care for the sick, and comfort the bereaved, but as the President said: 'We want to be banded together in close brotherly union, and to strive by mutual counsels and mingled prayers to make each other better preachers.' As it was in the beginning, so it has continued to be all through the years.

More important than any of these things was the debate that arose on the Rule that every Officer of the Association must be an accredited local preacher. A breath of the blasts of controversy which were sweeping over the Connexion might have fluttered the serenity of the assembly at this point, but no acrimonious or angry word was spoken. Numbers of the brethren had suffered, or were about to suffer, excommunication from the parent body for the side they had taken in the current disputes, and they feared for their standing in the Association. Sanctified sagacity was displayed by the leaders. Here was a rock on which the Association's vessel might have foundered and sunk, had not a straight and safe course been steered by the men at the helm. They urged that the expelled brethren were still local preachers, and as such could be members and hold office in the branches, but as a Wesleyan Association its recognized executive officers ought not to be other than accredited Wesleyans. They succeeded in deferring consideration of the matter for a year, and meanwhile the Rule was to stand. It was a triumph of far-seeing statesmanship, and the President had good reason for exclaiming: 'I see the hand of God in it; you have saved the Association.'

Francis Pearson again declined nomination for the Chair, and himself proposed the election of the Hon. Secretary, Isaac English, who received a unanimous vote. He was at once inducted by the outgoing President, whose retirement was signalized by the singing of a hymn to the tune of *Auld Lang Syne*. This hymn had been written by a Bristol local preacher named G. Pocock, for use by a gathering of his old friends and preachers on the day when the Centenary of 1839 was being celebrated. It is said to have moved to tears those who sang it first, and as our founding fathers counted it worthy of adoption, it may fittingly find a place in this record:

Should old acquaintance be forgot,
And never brought to mind?
No, brethren, no, true friendship's knot
Time never can unbind.

CHORUS

Time never can unbind, dear friends, etc.

The sweet remembrance of the past,
Which kindred spirits share,
Shall live as long as heaven shall last,
And spread a banquet there.

How good and pleasant thus to dwell
In unity and love;
Such unction once on Zion fell,
Such dew from heaven above.

Such dew, such unction, still descend,
In showers e'en now they fall;
Pass, pass the token of a friend
(taking hold of each other's hands)
For we are brethren all.

Thus joined in spirit, hand-in-hand,
Still let us walk below,
Like Wesley's first delightful band,
A hundred years ago.

And when the Source of this bright grace
Requires this fleeting breath,
True friendship then shall find a place
Beyond the verge of death.

With all its defects, the hymn has the marrow of true feeling in it, and with some revision might be brought into service again. The last act of this first Aggregate Meeting was to pass a resolution deploring the disturbed state of the Connexion, resolving to exercise with zeal, diligence, and faithfulness the various functions of their ministry and official positions, and to labour unceasingly for the revival of the work of God, and praying for the outpouring of the Holy Ghost upon the Connexion, that all causes of strife, division, and offence might be removed. In the Association there were no parties or factions then, nor ever have there been. These men were not the troublers of Israel; they worked peaceably together in their beloved fellowship of service, and their desire and prayer was for the peace of the Church. 'Whatever record leap to light, they never shall be shamed.' They were traduced and accused of evil designs, but it is their traducers who today are convicted of ill will and false witness.

It only remains to add that William Harris was elected as Hon. Secretary in the new President's place, and that Dr. Melson again preached the official sermon, his text being Genesis 6, 4: 'There were giants in the earth in those days.' This time the discourse extended to two hours and a half, which argues in himself and his hearers resources of physical strength and endurance not much inferior to the men of might referred to in the good doctor's text.

In accordance with the previous year's proposal, the Aggregate Meeting of 1851, held in Sheffield, printed a 'Plan' of services and meetings. It was not at all like the attractive and comprehensive handbooks which have been produced of late years. It consisted of a single sheet giving the names of the preachers and preaching-places on the Sunday, and announcing the various meetings on the three following days. These included prayer-meetings at 7 a.m.; a General Committee meeting at 8 a.m.; a Love-feast on Sunday afternoon; the annual sermon by the President, Isaac English, at 10.30 a.m. on Monday; a Tea Meeting of 870 guests (tickets for the tea were one shilling, but threepence was accounted sufficient for persons to pay to hear the after-tea speeches); and the Lord's Supper, at which the minister was assisted by senior local preachers. The Sheffield friends gave the brethren 'a thoroughly Methodist welcome, of the good old Yorkshire kind', but the use of the Wesleyan chapels was refused by the circuit officials. After the cordial kindness of the President of the Conference and the ministers in London and Birmingham, this was an unkind blow. But the brethren wasted no time in complaining. They took what they could get from others more kindly disposed, such as Independents, Baptists, and other branches of the Methodist family. The 'Plan' of places and preachers prepared beforehand differs in a few respects from the list as given in the Magazine report of the Aggregate Meeting. This was doubtless due to those late changes which have been the bane of plan-makers from time immemorial. Here is the first recorded list of services at an Aggregate Meeting:

	10.30 a.m.	6 p.m
Music Hall, Surrey St.	Wm. Harris, London	J. B. Melson, M.D., Birmingham
Athenæum, Surrey St.	T. Somersides, Ambergate	F. Felvus, Stourport
Coalpit Lane Chapel	J. Jebson, Huddersfield	—
Mount Tabor Chapel	James Taylor, Barnsley	J. R. Brown, London
Eyre Street Chapel	J. Towne, Melton Mowbray	—
South Street Chapel	Richard Carter, Buckingham	—

	10.30 a.m.	6 p.m.
Park Rooms	Francis Pearson, Birmingham	J. K. Hardy, Birmingham
Surrey Street Chapel	J. H. Taylor, London	H. Pogson, Huddersfield
Howard Street Chapel	D. Holdsworth, Ashton-under-Lyne	Isaac Marsden, Doncaster
Lee Croft Chapel	—	J. H. Carr, Leeds
Nether Chapel, Norfolk Street	—	W. B. Carter, Nottingham
Port Mahon Chapel	—	J. B. Andrews, Grindleford Bridge
Queen Street Chapel	—	W. Nelstrop, Pontefract
Townhead Street	—	T. Chamberlain, Windsor

The year of the Great Exhibition in Hyde Park, 1851, drew many people from the provinces to inspect its wonders. To the expense incurred in such travelling was partly attributed a smaller attendance at the Aggregate Meeting than was expected. As it was, nearly three hundred were present, and much good work was done. In the preceding February the General Committee had been made aware of brethren in distress due to causes other than 'sickness'. To relieve these cases, a superannuation allowance of 2*s.* 6*d.* a week was approved. This venturousness was not only heartily endorsed by the Aggregate Meeting, but it went still further, and resolved that the sum should be increased to 4*s.* a week. It was realized that this measure would require to be sustained by the liberality of the friends of local preachers and the Association, but they felt that 'the venerable men who have spent their best energies in the service of the Church' ought not to 'be abandoned to legal charity and the forbidding associations of a Union House'. Another step forward was the allowance to a brother of £4 on the death of his wife, though it was cannily ruled that the sum would be deducted from the £8 due on the brother's own decease. It is interesting to note that at this meeting the Hon. Secretary threw out the idea of erecting Alms-houses for poor old local preachers. Several contributions were promised toward this object when it should be started, but it remained only an idea and a dream. Now, after a hundred years, the vision is reborn, and hopes are high of 'Mutual Aid' homes for the sick and aged becoming a glad and blessed reality.

The prickly problem left over from last year of deciding who were to be regarded as local preachers in view of the current divisions, and so eligible for membership in the Association, was solved with common sense, and almost with unanimity, only two voting against the following resolution:

That the words 'Wesleyan Methodist local preachers' and 'accredited local preachers' occurring in the rules, shall not be taken in such sense as to exclude those persons who, in the present afflicted state of Methodism, are connected with the Branch Societies.

Thus was the unity preserved both of the Association and of the brotherhood of Methodist local preachers. In view of the fierceness of the controversies raging around them, and the high feelings aroused, it appears a veritable miracle of grace that these men should have avoided disputations which would have wrecked their newly launched bark, and built a wall of partition between brethren in Christ. The organ of the authorities, the *Watchman*, attacked the resolution with malignant force. A dignified reply was made by William B. Carter (President) and William Harris (Hon. Secretary). They pointed out that the Association was still limited, as its name indicates, to 'Wesleyan Methodist Local Preachers'. It was admitted that the Association declined to endorse 'the acts of those who, on account of ecclesiastical differences, have cast out of our Connexion persons who until recently were united with us'. But, it was pointed out, the resolution referred to the 'afflicted state of Methodism', and the Association desired to maintain a neutral position as between the Conference and the Reformers, 'believing that the claims of our afflicted brethren are paramount to those of a disputable policy, and that the rights of humanity ought not to be suspended upon the will or judgement of any man or order of men whatever'. That was nobly said, and it is a worthy revelation of the stuff of which our fathers in Israel were made. As they were independent of Conference, so they would be free from partisan entanglements. At no period of its history did the Association rank itself with any of the conflicting parties. It was conceived before the disruptive Conference of 1849 was held, and came into being too soon after to be regarded as the offspring of revolution. Richard Chew, in his biography of the Rev. James Everett, says: 'But for the Reform movement, no such fund would have existed.' Mr. Chew protests too much. The ship was designed and framed on the stocks before the storm broke, and when it was launched, it kept an even keel and a steady course because its navigators refused to look to the right or left, but only steered straight on.

The confidence of the brethren in the rightness of their cause, and the necessity of the work to which they had set their hand, was confirmed by the figures given in their second Annual Report. The number of members had grown to 1,806, an increase of 546. Of these, 132 were honorary members, not being local preachers. Sick cases numbering 107 had been relieved, at a cost of £193. Death allowances amounted to £88, and annuities to £58. The income was derived mainly from members' entrance fees (£223) and subscriptions (£822), and a sum of £164 from 'free' subscriptions from sympathizing friends. £500 was invested in Consols, and after sundry expenses had been paid, including the Secretary's salary of £70 15*s*., the balance in the Treasurer's hands was £214. The capital account shows that the entire property of the Association on 15th September 1851 was £1,964. Not much to boast about, perhaps, but the 'infant of days' was living and growing. In these 'seeds of weak beginnings' lay 'intreasured' a harvest of joy and blessing beyond the brightest dreams of those who ploughed and planted.

CHAPTER FOUR

MORE AND MORE IT SPREADS AND GROWS

REFERENCE has been made in the previous pages to the hostility shown in some quarters to the existence and the activities of the Association. The most vocal and violent of its opposers were to be found among the ministers. This was perhaps only to be expected when the nature and course of the disputes agitating the Connexion are considered. It would serve no good purpose to revive these ancient controversies now, or to dwell at length on the bitter attacks to which the nascent society was subject. Ministerial opposition was by no means universal, and the friendliness and sympathy of the Presidents of Conference and other ministers in the early days has already been noted. But the story of the Association would be incomplete if the 'darts envenomed' hurled by its foes were ignored. One instance may be given as typical of the rest, and then we can consign this unhappy topic to oblivion.

A penny monthly journal called *The Wesleyan Vindicator and Constitutional Methodist*, edited by the Rev. Samuel Jackson, published in its issue for December 1851 an editorial on the 'Local Preachers Mutual Aid Association'. It was 'with considerable reluctance', and from 'nothing but a sense of duty', that the detestable thing was noticed at all in the pages of this chaste periodical, but in the interests of 'our brethren the local preachers' it was necessary 'to point out some of those false steps which will eventually lead to its own destruction'. 'Its object *professedly* was to give pecuniary relief to *Wesleyan Methodist* local preachers, being members of the Association, whom sickness or age had incapacitated for their regular daily avocations' (the *italics* are the editor's). This was a 'praiseworthy intention', but 'it was a matter for grave consideration whether, in a Connexion like our own, the project could be satisfactorily carried out'. There is something queer about this invidious dubiety. One would have thought that, 'in a Connexion like our own', whose founder had urged his followers to 'do all possible good, of every possible kind, to all men', such a benevolent brotherhood would be heartily welcomed and supported. No reason is given for this dismal presage other than the ruling that local preachers in connexion with 'Branch Societies' were not to be excluded from membership in the Association. The writer admits that 'several honoured and greatly respected names are to be found on the list of subscribers' and he is terribly anxious to divert support from an Association 'which so *directly* and *intentionally* countenances the present assault upon Methodism'. The *italics* are again the editor's, but how far from the truth are his words will be evident to all impartial readers of our previous chapters.

The editor of the *Vindicator* next turns his critical artillery against the accounts. Because only one-sixth of the income for the first two years has been expended on the relief of its members, he asserts that the design for which the Association was established has not been fulfilled, 'nor do we see any prospect of that design being fulfilled in time to come'. The prudent investment of the bulk of the funds wins no commendation from him, and the expenditure on the Secretary's salary (£70), on the Magazine (£300), and on printing and stationery (£70), is held to be unjustified. At the same time, he forecasts that the raising of the superannuated members' allowances from 2*s*. 6*d*. per week to 4*s*. will leave the Association next year 'minus between £50 and £60, with nothing for the funds', and he asks: 'Does this look very inviting?' He begs the local preachers to consider whether such an Association 'is worthy of their countenance and support'. 'We have seen that it is utterly anti-Wesleyan in its intentions and practice; and that it gives direct countenance to men who assail our common and much-loved Methodism.' With which parting barb, poisoned with untruth, he concludes his fantastic diatribe.

Happy and well was it for thousands of our needy and afflicted brothers and sisters that his attempts to strangle the new-born child were all in vain. It lived and thrived, and his prophecies of gloom and doom survive only to his own discomfiture.

Who, by aspersions, throw a stone
At the head of others, hit their own.

The onslaught of the *Vindicator* naturally elicited a counterblast in the Association's magazine, but this taking up of the gage met with strong disapproval in the Aggregate Meeting at Huddersfield the next year. These brotherly-minded men, like the true Methodists they were, wanted to be 'the friends of all and the enemies of none'.

The President insisted that the Association was a *neutral* institution, and Josiah Carr, of Leeds, put the case with Yorkshire bluntness and good sense; 'Take no notice of either party, and we shall get on all the better'. Which was what the brethren resolved to do, and have done ever since. For 'names and sects and parties' in Church or State the Mutual Aid Association has never contended. It has had one object in view, and has pursued it with singleness of purpose. The Rev. Samuel

Jackson has had many successors whose wishes and words have been ill-disposed toward us, nor is their tribe entirely extinct. But though the Association has never sought official recognition, the disinterestedness of its aims, and the devoted zeal of its agents, have won the sympathies of the Methodist people, and among the ministers we are thankful to number some of our best and most helpful friends.

The official Report presented to the Huddersfield annual meeting in 1852 showed a net increase of 836 members. The total was now 2,642, of whom 231 were honorary members. The sum of £1,225 had been expended in benefits, nearly four times as much as in the previous year. The income had grown to £2,860; another £1,000 was invested in Consols; the Magazine cost £482, against which could be set sales amounting to £323; and the Secretary's salary had gone up to £95.

With a capital account of £2,739 as the result of three years working, Samuel Jackson's solicitous fears and prognostications of the Association's speedy demise were seen to be the baseless fancies of one whose wish was father to his thought. Despite the antagonisms, the slanders, and the obstacles placed in its path, the Association won its widening way as year followed year. From the first the brethren were prepared to abide by the Scriptural test: 'If this work be of men, it will be overthrown; but if it is of God, ye will not be able to overthrow them.' God's blessing prospered the faith and devotion of his servants, and in that sign they toiled on and triumphed.

It is impossible within the compass of this volume to record in detail the activities and progress of each succeeding year. We can only attempt a swift and summary survey, making mention as occasion serves of any

JUDGE SAMUEL D. WADDY, B.A., Q.C., M.P.

President 1870

salient and significant feature. It was in the Leeds Aggregate Meeting of 1853 that the payment to disabled and necessitous brethren was fixed at 8*s.* a week for the first six months, 4*s.* for the second six months, and 2*s.* 6*d.* as long as the necessity continued. These amounts remained in force unchanged for ninety years, until the Aggregate Meeting in 1943 raised the payments for the respective periods to 16*s.*, 8*s.*, and 5*s.* The Leeds Meeting also decided to change the date for the annual assembly to June, as a more attractive season of the year than October, and this precedent has become a good and happy custom. The Annual Report presented at Leeds was distinguished by the announcement of the first legacy bequeathed to the Association. The testator was Mr. Tapp, of Oakhill, near Bath. His name deserves to be recorded with honour, as being the first of a great host of friends who have generously remembered the Association in this way. It is interesting to note that the expenses of this Aggregate Meeting amounted to only £41 4*s.* 10*d.*, and the receipts from collections, sale of tickets, and of what are quaintly termed 'spared provisions', realized £47 3*s.* 3½*d.*

In 1854 the Aggregate Meeting met in St. Martin's Hall, Long Acre, London, with James Wild, the enthusiastic and ever generous Treasurer, as President; in 1855 it went to Bristol; and in 1856 to Sheffield for the second time. Only eleven places of worship opened their pulpits to the Association's representatives, and the Report showed an adverse balance of £94 on the year's working. Sick members numbering 408 had been relieved at a cost of £874, funeral allowances were granted to a total of £338, and 101 annuitants had received £909, 65 of them having 4*s.* a week, and the remainder 3*s.* or less. The Rule confining honorary membership to persons not being local preachers had been relaxed, and 200 of the 500 honorary members were local preachers.

The 1857 Aggregate Meeting in Louth is notable for the recognition given by name for the first time to the Wesleyan Reformers. This momentous amendment was debated long and seriously, and it was ultimately carried by a majority of three to one in the following form:

> That this Association shall consist of accredited local preachers in Great Britain who belong to the Wesleyan-Methodist Connexion, the Branch Societies of the Wesleyan Reformers and Wesleyan Association Methodists.

A chronicler in the Magazine calls this settlement 'an important epoch in the history of the Mutual Aid Association'. It was scarcely that. As has been already seen, the Rule as amended had always been the practice. Eight years had passed, and it was obvious that those who had 'gone out' were not likely to return, but were vigorously consolidating their position. The broken fragments were coming together and finding strength in union. The Wesleyan Association, the Protestant Methodists, and the Arminian Methodists had become one body, and in 1857, at Rochdale, this amalgamation was joined by a large section of the Reformers, the resultant communion being known as the 'United Methodist Free Churches'. Therefore the amended Rule changed nothing, but openly acknowledged the 'accreditedness' of their brother local preachers in other branches of the Wesleyan family, and their eligibility for membership in the Association. It was a sound and sagacious thing to do, and although time has brought other changes in the Rule, the name of the Wesleyan Reform Union still remains to witness to the integral part played by its members from the beginning in the long history of the Association.

So the years pass, bringing to these ministering servants of the poor, as to all things living, mingled shade and sunshine. The Association did not find it 'roses, roses, all the way'. Few were the 'Conference' chapels which would permit the men of the Mutual Aid to make an appeal from their pulpits; in the five years 1856-60 the membership fell from 2,940 to 2,441; and the annual income, averaging round about £2,500, left so little margin over expenditure, that in 1857 £500 worth of Stock had to be realized. In view of the prosperity of later years it is well to remember the 'growing pains' of adolescence. Our fathers contended with adversity in reliance on God. He honoured their faith and singleness of heart, and the fruits of their labours are enjoyed by their succeeding race. 'We went through fire and through water, but Thou broughtest us out into a place of abundance.'

To augment the funds in order to raise the annuities of brethren over 70 years old to 4*s*. a week, a bazaar was organized in connexion with the London Aggregate Meeting of June 1860. It was held in the Hanover Square Rooms, and all the Committee and business meetings took place on the same premises. The proceeds of the bazaar amounted to £1,296, and so many articles and goods remained over that a supplementary sale was arranged for July in Exeter Hall.

A more unusual method of raising funds was propounded by William Bowron in the annual public meeting of this year. He conceived the novel idea of asking a penny for each sermon he preached, holding the quaint notion that a sermon must be at least worth that modest sum. By this means he succeeded in collecting a goodly number of shillings during the year, and won for himself the soubriquet of the 'Penny Preacher'. Several brethren followed his example, and many pounds were raised annually in this way. It was an ingenious scheme, but a similar assessment of the value of our sermons might not meet with such an appreciative response in modern times. At any rate, few local preachers would be daring enough to try it.

Also in 1860, in the May number of the *Local Preachers' Magazine*, appeared a piece of writing which was to become famous in Association circles for many a year. This was a 'Lesson in Parable', called 'Grandfather Johnson, the Old Local Preacher', by an author who wrote under the pseudonym 'Alma'. It was the story of a grave and reverend grandsire whose declining years were spent in the home of a widowed daughter. When the old man grew too feeble to work, this gallant woman toiled many an eighteen-hours day to keep her father and her three fatherless children from seeking for parochial relief. At last the burden grew too great, means were almost exhausted, and one day the dread words were spoken: '*Grandfather must go.*' But ere the gates of the Union Workhouse opened to receive him, an angel of light appeared in the person of the postman, bringing a letter from the General Secretary of the Mutual Aid Association to say the the Committee had awarded the old saint 'an annuity of *four shillings* a week'. The author's italics indicate the astonishment caused by such munificence, and he graphically describes the joy and thankfulness that this bounty caused in the hearts and home of these humble folk. The story was published as a pamphlet at the price of one penny, and thousands of copies were sold. Its aim, said the author, was 'to provoke the Methodist people to the performance of an act of justice to their local preachers'. It certainly served to awaken many to a consciousness of what they owed to these men when in necessity, for the simple tale was founded on fact. Four shillings a week scarcely errs on the side of extravagance, but even that allowance gave rise to anxious doubts about the strain on the funds in those days. The award was indeed a venture of faith, and it is thanks to the courage of these pioneers that Methodism was freed from the shame of allowing its aged, destitute, and afflicted local preachers to depend on parish relief, or to end their days in the workhouse.

The year 1862 saw the beginning of the practice of sending a copy of the Magazine to honorary members, and in this year, too, it was decided to provide a Bible in which Presidents should inscribe their names. It was thought that 'with good bindings, clasps, etc.' such a Bible would be 'a nice heirloom for the Association', and the ceremony of presenting it each year would 'be a beautiful one'. This Bible has become an historic institution, and its presentation each year to the incoming President is always a moving moment in the ceremonial of induction.

Fifteen years had now passed, and a summary of the work done and the benefits conferred from 1848 to 1863 is a record of steady and sturdy growth. The membership was doubled, a total of £30,966 had been raised, £22,098 had been disbursed in benevolent payments, and £3,928 had been invested. It must now have become apparent to all that their brotherhood of compassion had come to stay. Inasmuch as it was caring for the needy and afflicted, it was doing service to the King of love who called them 'these My brethren'. From the beginning, His blessing rested abundantly upon this band of brothers, and He guided and 'led them safely, so that they feared not'.

CHAPTER FIVE

THE YEARS OF JUBILEE

WHEN JAMES WILD died on 1st May 1866, at the ripe age of 83, the Association lost one of its most devoted servants. From the first he had been an eager co-operator and an ardent campaigner in its behalf, and he spared neither time, nor strength, nor money to further its interests. His sympathy and love for his needy brethren sprang from his love for his Lord, and he was as zealous a preacher of the Word as he was a champion of the poor. A woollen merchant of some wealth, he was a generous supporter of Methodist causes. His sympathies were with Free Methodism, but he never left the old Wesleyan body, and accepted his quarterly ticket of membership to the last. Near his home at North End, Fulham, he built a handsome chapel, named 'Ebenezer', and he also established and supported at his own expense a day school in the same area. But the Mutual Aid Association and his fellow local preachers were ever foremost in his affection, and his generosity was unstinted in their support. His monetary contributions were frequent, and many an impoverished brother was indebted to him for the payment of his entrance fee and annual subscription. He was the Honorary Treasurer of the Association from the beginning until his death, and was elected President in 1854. His name will be remembered in ever grateful honour for his donation of £1,000 as an investment to provide our annuitants with an annual Christmas gift, or to use his own lovely phrase, 'to mend their Christmas cheer'. The James Wild Fund is an enduring monument to one to whom the Association owes much. For some time John Carter, of Kensington, had been assisting James Wild in the duties of Treasurer, and he now succeeded to the office.

When the brethren assembled in Ashton-under-Lyne in 1868, it is of interest to note that the Report describes the gathering as the 'Twentieth Meeting of Representatives, being the Nineteenth Annual Meeting'. This should have settled the vexed question of numbering the Aggregate Meetings referred to on a previous page, but the error crept in again the following year when the assembly at King's Cross, London, in 1869, was styled the 'Twenty-first Annual Meeting'. This meeting was noteworthy for the election to the General Committee of Samuel Danks Waddy, barrister-at-law, to be better known later as Judge Waddy. So swiftly appreciated were his gifts that at the next year's meeting in Gold Street Chapel, Northampton, Samuel Waddy was chosen as President. During this meeting W. B. Carter opened a discussion on 'Mutual Help for Mutual Improvement'. The Report runs: 'No resolution was taken, for it was not deemed advisable to mix up in any way the subject of the education of the local preachers with the one object of the Association, viz., the relief in sickness and old age of the necessitous local preachers.' More than seventy years later, when assistance in the education and training of local preachers was urged upon the Association's executive, the same attitude was adopted. Opinions may differ on the wisdom of this decision, but there is undoubted strength in singleness of purpose. 'This one thing I do' has ever been the mark of the Association, and therein lies in large measure the secret of its progress.

When the Aggregate Meeting went to Keighley in

1871, we are told that many of the brethren 'did not know how to pronounce its name rightly, or when pronounced they knew not the spelling of it'. But they found there 'a Sabbath-keeping, law-abiding, and God-fearing people . . . their forms erect, and tall and strong, and their faces blooming with health and beauty', though their speech 'sounds broad and rather harsh to the ear'. President Waddy preached in Temple Street Wesleyan and Cavendish Street U.M.F. Chapels on the Sunday. He could not stay for the Monday meetings, and in a letter to the Hon. Secretary suggested Easter as a more convenient season for the annual assembly. His presidential journeys at his own expense during the year had cost him £50, a sum which many Presidents in later times would regard as modest. He added a plea for the discontinuance of the President's sermon: 'It has been a sad trial and trouble to me.' Presidents in modern days are subject to trials and stresses of which Samuel Waddy knew nothing, but at least they are spared the ordeal of delivering an official sermon.

The death of Edward Creswell in September 1872 bereaved the Association of another of its most active originators and one of its earliest officials. He acted as Honorary Secretary until the Rules were adopted and printed, and his first minute book ran to one hundred pages quarto written in his own hand. At the first Aggregate Meeting, in 1850, he was unanimously elected General Secretary. The salary was only £80 a year, and the Secretary had to find his own office, and devote himself entirely to the interest of the Association. He obtained, so it is recorded, 'a pious and sensible wife' and laboured diligently in the Chelsea and Hammersmith circuits, in both of which he was a local preacher, class-leader, and chapel steward. Ill health compelled his removal from Knightsbridge to Mitcham, where 'the fresh country air, impregnated at times with the sweet scents of fields of lavender, roses, peppermint, and other herbs', revived him. That was in 1861. Eight years later he was stricken with paralysis, and lay bed-ridden for more than three years. He never complained, but counted it a mercy to have a bed to lie upon. He learned to write with his left hand, and kept his account books to the end of his life. As he could not attend committee meetings, he relinquished a quarter of his salary, though his resources were much straitened. A man of sterling Christian character, Edward Creswell gave of his best to all his work for God, and not least to the duties of his office as General Secretary. 'All the local secretaries and treasurers throughout England and Wales know how prompt he was in replying to correspondents, how clear and ample in explaining the points put before him, and how persistent in pressing the claims of the Association in localities where its cause appeared to languish.' So a contemporary testified of him, and the tradition of devoted efficiency created by Edward Creswell has been carried on by his successors in this most responsible office.

In 1873 the Aggregate Meeting chose George Sims from a long list of candidates to fill the vacant post of General Secretary.

So we come to 1874, the Silver Jubilee year of the Association. No trumpet sounded to proclaim the event, no flags or fireworks saluted the occasion. The brethren in Aggregate Meeting assembled 'kept the noiseless tenor of their way', content with such things as they had.

Yet they might have boasted a little as they looked back on the past quarter of a century. The hopes and fears, the toils and prayers, the faith and devotion which had attended the birth and nurture of the Association had produced a plant of sturdy growth, rooted firm and deep in the favour of God and the love of the Methodist people.

The Aggregate Meeting was held in Grosvenor Street Wesleyan Chapel, Manchester. One hundred and ten delegates from other districts attended, together with a number of local brethren. Preaching services were conducted in fifty-eight chapels, with a number of open-air meetings in addition. One enthusiastic brother, after taking his appointed Sunday work, gave three more addresses in the open air before the day was done. A platform had been put up for the officials on the Monday, but they declined the elevation, and took their seats below among their brethren. 'O what an age of golden days', when the 'platform' met on a common level with the 'floor'!

The membership was reported as 2,370, of whom 530 were honorary and 1,840 benefit members, an increase of seventy-eight and seventy respectively on the preceding year. On sickness and deaths the expenditure was £814, and on 113 annuitants £1,113. None of these last received more than 4*s.* a week. One brother, aged 85 years, having been placed in a local alms-house, wrote that he thought he could now do with one shilling a week less. Briefly, but beautifully, the Report comments in the true Mutual Aid Spirit: '*Your Committee however did not think so.*' The working expenses amounted to £252, including the Secretary's salary and postages, the cost of Magazines supplied to honorary members, printing, and stationery. No rent had to be paid for an office, which was lent by an ex-President, William Jameson. The total income for the year was £3,001, the highest in the Association's history, with the exception of 1861, the year of the Hanover Square bazaar. As a surety for the future, the goodly sum of £5,700 Consols was invested in the names of the Trustees; and the total amount distributed since first the work began was:

	£.	s.	d.
For sickness	17,222	7	10
For deaths	9,209	16	4
For annuities	20,187	1	6
Total to May 19th, 1874	46,619	5	8

These facts and figures are eloquent evidence of the need of the beneficent work the Association was doing, and of its growing stability and resources. More and more churches and congregations were becoming acquainted with the objects and spirit of the movement, and the better they knew it, the more they appreciated it, and opened their hands and hearts to help. The Silver Jubilee stock-taking must have afforded great encouragement for the future, but few of those who met in the 'metropolis of cotton' on that warm June day in 1874 can have imagined the greater things yet to be.

Up to this date the benefits of the Association had been confined to local preachers only, and no provision was made for their wives when the bread-winner was taken. It is not surprising that this omission was felt to bear hardly on those to whose comfort and care in the home the brethren owed so much, and whose love and sympathy and sacrifice supported them so unfailingly as they went forth to their appointments Sunday by Sunday. So in the Aggregate Meeting at City Road, London, in 1875 the following new Rule was 'with but few dissentients' adopted: 'The General Committee shall have power, in case of extreme poverty, to allow the widows of local preachers, deceased members of the Association, a weekly sum not exceeding 2*s*. 6*d*.' History does not relate why these 'dissentients' objected to this modest proposal. They were not of the Mutual Aid spirit, and they can be 'left unthought of in obscurity'. It is pleasing to note that even the phrase 'extreme poverty' was soon felt to be too harsh, and the softer rendering of 'necessitous circumstances' substituted.

The public meeting in connexion with this Aggregate Meeting was held in City Road Chapel, and was presided over by Mr. W. Shepherd Allen, M.P. for Newcastle-under-Lyme. One of the speakers was the Rev. Dr. Jobson, who not only commended the order of lay preachers, but in the name of all his ministerial brethren wished the Association God-speed, and confirmed the sincerity of his goodwill by a contribution of £10. This gesture is noteworthy as being a symptom of the friendlier attitude of the ministers toward the Association and its activities. Another example of this occurred at a meeting in Hebron Chapel, Bedminster, Bristol, in the following year when the Rev. E. D. Green warmly advocated the claims of the Association, and recited the following verses he had specially composed for the occasion:

Many greetings from Hebron to you we present,
The Mutual Aid workers, on kindly work bent;
And while wishing your funds and your ranks may increase,
We will pray that God's favour to you may not cease.

Too long have our churches their 'locals' ignored,
Or coldly received them, and this we've deplored;
But happily now they are taking a grade,
That while higher, is warmer, by this Mutual Aid.

Our brethren to frailty and weakness are prone,
And strangers they are not to tears and a moan;
But when sickness and want shall their dwellings invade,
Small relief they may gain from their own Mutual Aid.

Not great poetry perhaps, but worthy of record as a warm-hearted tribute of friendliness.

Many further instances of ministerial cordiality might be mentioned. Two will suffice to show how the climate was changing. At Sheffield in 1881 the Rev. David Barley, superintendent of the Carver Street Circuit, said:

'Who could find fault with the Local Preachers Mutual Aid Association?' He was glad to know that it was not drooping or dying out, and he trusted that it would have yet greater vivacity and power. And at City Road in 1885, the Rev. Austin Davey, one of the circuit ministers, said that the great fault of the Association was that it was too modest! 'Thus the whirligig of time brings in his revenges', and the vindictive vapourings of Samuel Jackson's *Vindicator* are seen in retrospect as the senseless effusion of ignorance and ill will.

So stable and assured was the position of the Association now that the General Committee was directed to take Counsel's opinion, and 'to adopt any means necessary with a view to giving legal security to the investment and use of our funds in accordance with the present design of our Association'. In pursuance of this instruction, the draft of 'a Deed of Trust, which may be deemed our Foundation Deed', was presented to the York Aggregate Meeting of 1880. The Deed was printed in full in the next issue of the *Local Preachers' Magazine*. The Trustees named were Richard Carter, of Buckingham, Thomas Chamberlain, of Windsor, William Willmer Pocock, of Wandsworth, and John Carter, of Chelsea, and they were 'possessed of or entitled to a sum of £9,800, £3 per centum Consolidated Bank Annuities', which was the considerable amount to which the assets of the Association had grown. This Deed was duly signed and executed on 24th November 1881.

The Sheffield Aggregate Meeting in 1881 was shadowed by the absence, through illness, of the Honorary Secretary, Thomas Chamberlain. For thirty years he had been a regular attendant, and for more than twenty years had served as Secretary 'in that efficient manner that can never be surpassed', as the Report expresses it. In view of his affliction, it was deemed wise to appoint a colleague to share the duties of the secretariat, and the lot fell on A. Russell Johnson, who occupied this high office with dignity and devotion until his death in 1902.

In November 1882 the Association sustained a severe loss by the death of its General Secretary, George Sims. For more than fifty years he had been a member of the Wesleyan Methodist Connexion, for nearly forty years he was a local preacher, class-leader, and office bearer in the Hinde Street Circuit, London, and had been Secretary of the Association for ten years. He was 'greatly beloved and deeply lamented'. Before the General Committee proceeded to fill the vacancy it passed a resolution that it was not desirable to elect as General Secretary any brother who was a member of the General Committee, and this regulation was adopted by the Aggregate Meeting in the same year. The post was advertised in the *Methodist Recorder* and the *Methodist*, and forty-four applications were received. A short list was selected, and by a unanimous vote, John Harding, of Clapham, was appointed on 10th January 1883 at a salary of £130 a year, payable quarterly, increased by more or less regular increments of £10. For this scant recompense the Association secured the services of a man who was to serve it for thirty years with faithful care, performing his duties with undeviating fidelity and diligence, and enhancing his ministry with the graces and winsomeness of a true Christian gentleman.

In its December meeting in the year 1882 the General Committee sent a message of congratulation to S. D. Waddy, Q.C., now one of the Association's Trustees, on his election as a Member of Parliament for Edinburgh; and it also fixed on Newcastle-on-Tyne for the annual meeting in 1883. This Aggregate Meeting was held in Wesley Chapel, Prudhoe Street, and was notable for the election as President of Alderman William Haswell Stephenson, whose distinguished services to the Association were recognized thirteen years later by his election to a second term of office in the Chair. In his inaugural address, he proudly declared that he was a Methodist of the fourth generation on both sides of the house, and that he and all his family went to class every week. Near where the brethren were meeting was the Orphan House, for the site of which John Wesley had given his great-grandfather two shillings per square yard. Among the elections to the General Committee at this Aggregate Meeting the names appear of two brethren destined to win particular honour and affection for long and loyal service in after years—George Johnson, of Faversham, and J. Wesley Walker, of Maidenhead.

In 1885 the Aggregate Meeting again met in City Road, London, The growing interest in the Association's work was evidenced by an attendance of nearly three hundred brethren, and by the notice given to it in the *Methodist Recorder* and the *Methodist Times*, the latter paper having published an interview with the President, A. Russell Johnson. The appointment of J. Bamford Slack, of Ripley, as Secretary of the meeting introduces another name which became famous in our history. Owing to his continued illness, Thomas Chamberlain had found it necessary to resign the office of Honorary Secretary, and with his wife and family, consisting of eight children all under 18, was removing to New Zealand. He had been a great servant of the Association, and his departure evoked many tributes to his personal worth and valued services. He was elected Honorary Secretary first in 1854, again in 1855, and again in 1861, and held the position continuously from that date. In 1856 he was called to the Chair as President, and he became a Trustee in 1860. He had also been Alderman and Mayor of the Borough of Windsor, and his labours for the public good were recognized by a gift of £300, and a testimonial signed by Prince and Princess Christian and leading citizens. A zealous and loyal officer, and a wise and prudent administrator, Thomas Chamberlain is worthy of grateful honour for his sound guidance and leadership during the formative years of the Association. He died in New Zealand in 1889, aged 70. It was proposed that a sum of two hundred guineas should be contributed out of the funds to a proposed parting gift to Chamberlain, but the brethren discreetly decided that money subscribed for the needy ought not to be diverted in this way. A testimonial fund of £500 was raised by his friends and fellow-members.

By a unanimous vote, A. Russell Johnson and M. L. Clapham, of Bayswater, were appointed as the new Honorary Secretaries.

In passing, it is worthy of note that this Aggregate Meeting affords striking evidence of the growing good-will of the ordained ministry toward the Association and all its works. The annual sermon was preached in Great Queen Street Chapel by the President of the Conference, the Rev. F. Greeves, D.D. The annual public meeting was held in the City Temple, and was presided over by Dr. Joseph Parker, whose eloquent and fervent address to his 'fellow preachers' left his lay brethren in no doubt as to their apostolic authority. Another of the speakers was the popular Rev. Jackson Wray. It is no wonder that the meeting in that famous sanctuary was marked by the warmest enthusiasm. Another old ministerial friend was greeted with a welcoming cheer when the Rev. Joseph Hargreaves rose in the Aggregate Meeting, and recalled that he had given the address at the Sacramental Service in City Road Chapel on the memorable October evening in 1849, when the Association was brought to birth. The institution of the annual sermon, it may be mentioned, was due to a suggestion made by the Rev. Charles Garrett, who thought that in this way ministers in London for the May Meetings might show their practical sympathy with the Association and its work. At the invitation of the General Committee, Mr. Garrett preached the first of such sermons in 1884. Other famous preachers found in this service an opportunity to bless and help their lay colleagues in the ministry, the names of Hugh Price Hughes, Dr. W. L. Watkinson, Dr. T. B. Stephenson, and Mark Guy Pearse being sufficient to show that the occasion was accounted worthy of the best that Methodism could give. Truly, the Association was marching on.

A great step for the encouragement and consolidation of the work in the Districts was taken in 1886, when the Aggregate Meeting approved the appointment of a convener for each District. The office of convener has become so accustomed and indispensable a part of our organization that it is difficult to realize that it was not invented until nearly forty years had passed. Even then the Honorary Secretary pronounced the scheme superfluous and unworkable. To F. J. Littlewood, of Doncaster, belongs the honour of successfully urging this fruitful innovation on the Aggregate Meeting, although attempts had been made by others two or three years before. Among the first to be chosen for the new, and now historic, office of District Convener were such men of note as C. S. Madder (Bedford and Northampton), George Johnson (Kent), J. W. Laycock (Halifax), Moses Atkinson (Leeds), Hugh Wyatt (Lincoln), George Wain (York), and James Gilbert (First London). No specific duties and responsibilities were entrusted to conveners for a long time. They were merely to consult with the secretaries and two members of each Branch, and consider the state of the work. The constitution of District Committees was decided on in 1887, but it was not until six years later, in 1893, that the Rules for District Committees were adopted. These bodies were given the power and authority they have since possessed to the general profit and benefit. Even then, there were nervous heart-searchings at Headquarters, and the Association's solicitor had to be called in to reassure the fearful that no infraction of any law would be caused by this eminently sensible and useful proceeding. Conveners having been duly appointed, the following year, 1887, saw the beginning of the practice of presenting District Reports in the Aggregate Meeting, a practice which continued until the coming of the second World War compelled the cutting-down of the duration and the agenda of the Aggregate Meeting.

The year 1887 was the jubilee of Queen Victoria's reign, and an address of congratulation to Her Majesty was prepared, and signed by J. W. Laycock, the President, Moses Atkinson, the Ex-President, and the Honorary and General Secretaries. Memorials were also approved for presentation to the Conferences of the Wesleyan Methodist Church, of the Reformed Methodist Church, and of the United Methodist Free Church, praying for 'the gradual gathering together in one of all the families of our Methodist Israel'. This desire for reunion arose out of the practical experience of men who, though belonging to different branches of the Methodist Church, had been able to work together in the Mutual Aid Association for thirty-eight years, during which 'no instance of jealousy, unkindness, or partiality has ever occurred'. It was a big claim to make, but unity of spirit, 'the fellowship of heart and soul and mind', has ever marked and blessed this service of love from its earliest days. Fellowship has indeed been its strength and glory, and having found how good and pleasant it was for brethren to meet and work together, it is not surprising that this goodly fellowship of prophets should be among the first to voice the hope of reuniting the sundered members of the Methodist family.

The numbers of representatives attending the annual meetings naturally fluctuated from year to year, but the steadily increasing interest was beginning to create difficulties regarding hospitality and appointments. The attendance varied from fifty-four in 1873 to 348 in 1886. At the Hull meeting in 1893, John Broxap bluntly stated that the number of delegates attending the Aggregate Meeting was becoming too large, and it was getting to be too much of a good thing to provide homes for so many. The meeting agreed that action was necessary to deal with the problem, and passed a resolution that attendance henceforth should be by election of the Branches and not by individual option, and that the total number eligible to attend as representatives should be determined by the General Committee. References also appear to the dereliction of duty shown by appointed delegates who failed to come, and had not the courtesy to write a letter of explanation to their expectant hosts. This breach of good manners was condemned as a blot on the fair name of the brotherhood, but the like offence, unfortunately, is not unknown still.

Time's scythe had by now mown down many of the noble band of original founders and fathers of the Association. Richard Carter, a Trustee from 1850 and President in 1855, died in 1884; William Brown Carter, President in 1851 and one of the Editors of the Magazine, a scholarly and many-gifted man, passed away in June 1887; and in December of the same year died John Towne, who had been President in 1858.

Father Towne as he came to be called, was a member

of the first Committee elected in 1849, and remained a member till his death, at the age of 87. The branch at Melton Mowbray, from whence he hailed, was one of the earliest to be formed, and remains still in vigorous activity. Lovable, eloquent, and devoted, John Towne, so Russell Johnson writes, was a man 'whose face had heaven written on every feature, and whose very smile was a benediction'.

It is remarkable how many of these saints and servants of God were blessed with 'length of days and long life'. Of the first fifty Presidents, seventeen lived to be over 80 years of age, and two (John Carter and J. Wesley Walker) to be over 90. In 1890, when the Aggregate Meeting met in Central Hall, Corporation Street, Birmingham, Dr. Melson, who had preached the sermon at the meeting in 1849 when the Association was born, and who was one of the six original Trustees, was still alive, and a letter of fraternal greeting and gratitude was sent to him. There was a fitness in this remembrance of a Birmingham celebrity, for that city, though not the birthplace, was, in Shakespearian phrase, the 'procreant cradle' of the Association. In 1894, at Burslem, another of the early pioneers and former leaders appeared, William Harris, the first President, now elevated to the dignity of 'the reverend'. He presented the General Committee with a cheque for £10, expressed his pleasure that the travail and strife of other times had given place to peace and prosperity, and as a veteran of 81 prayed for blessing and success to attend the then President, J. Bamford Slack, who had come to the Chair at the age of 36.

So with the tide of Time, the tide of the Association's fortune flowed on, 'stilled and astir, and checked and never-ceasing'. In 1895, in Brunswick Chapel, Newcastle-on-Tyne, W. H. Stephenson, then serving a third term as Mayor of the city, was chosen as President of the Association for the second time, not without some deprecation of re-elections. An offer to co-operate gratuitously in the management and editorship of the Magazine had been received from a minister who was described as 'a literary gentleman of great experience'. This was so novel and strange an intrusion into this sodality of lay brothers that it may well have been viewed with mistrust. Happily, the counsels of wisdom prevailed, and the Rev. Isaac E. Page was appointed as co-Editor with J. Wesley Walker. Thus began a labour of love which was a joy and blessing to all for many years. The only minister who ever occupied an official position in the Association, the Rev. I. E. Page was the most brotherly and modest of colleagues, and his saintly spirit and sweetness of temper made his presence welcome and gracious at all times. It was at this Newcastle meeting that the Association first began to be honoured by deputations of greeting from Church and civic authorities. Ministers representing the Wesleyan Synod and the United Methodist Free Church spoke in appreciation of the Association's objects of self-help and benevolence, and the Mayor and Sheriff, in their regalia of office, presented a greeting in the name of the City.

As the Mayor was our good friend and brother, W. H. Stephenson, this part of the proceedings had a pleasant touch of intimacy. Reply to these august visitors was made by S. D. Waddy, Q.C., who thanked the ministers for the kind things they had said, adding softly, to the delight of the brethren: 'It was not always so.' So felicitous and able was the learned Counsel's speech, that one minister was heard to say to another: 'We have come here to learn how to speak.'

By this time, the practical benefits and spiritual

blessings enjoyed by those in membership with the Association were so unquestionable that brethren in other branches of Methodism began to view with longing this 'Canaan's goodly land'. Unfortunately, as to the Jews of old, a 'Jordan rolled between' in the shape of the Rules. A formal application for organic union having been received in 1891, on behalf of the local preachers of the Methodist New Connexion, the question was referred to the Association's solicitor, J. B. Ingle, and to Queen's Counsel, S. D. Waddy. The latter's opinion stated that the amalgamation could be effected if the Rules were altered in due form at the proper time. When, therefore, in 1895, a letter was received from the Rev. George Packer, the President of the Methodist New Connexion, inquiring whether and on what terms their local preachers could enter the Association, negotiations were begun in a cordial spirit, and in the Bolton Aggregate Meeting of 1896, the New Connexion brethren were made eligible for membership on payment of the sum of £1,500. The Conference of that body approved and adopted the proposal for union, and commended 'this desirable object to the generous sympathy of our circuits', and the entrance fee was paid out of money raised by a Centenary effort. Within a year, 300 out of the 1,203 New Connexion local preachers had availed themselves of the privilege thus opened to them, and one of the best known among them, Edwin Talbot, of Batley, became a member of the General Committee.

An incident of outstanding note occurred at this Bolton meeting when, for the first time in the history of the Association, the then President of the Wesleyan Conference, the Rev. D. J. Waller, D.D., appeared on the platform to express his sympathy with the work of local preachers and with the aims and activities of the Association. Dr. Waller made practical proof of his appreciation by announcing his desire to be enrolled as an honorary member.

When John Wesley Walker was elected as President in 1897 it was recorded that his connection with the Association was the direct result of reading Philip Parker's tract, *Grandfather Johnson.* The author of this famous publication had died just two years before his illustrious recruit attained the place of highest honour. He was within eight days of completing his ninety-second year when he passed away, and his long life was filled with fruitful service and good works. His memory deserves to be treasured among the most devoted of the Association's servants. Philip Parker was born in 1803 in a Sussex agricultural labourer's cottage, and when he was three years old his mother was left a widow with eleven children to care for. The boy got what education he could from such parish schools as there were, and began work on a farm at two shillings a week. He left the country for London at the age of 18, entered the book trade, and eventually became a local preacher and a class leader at Southwark Wesleyan Chapel. The Reform movement enlisted his wholehearted sympathies, and for this cause he was, as he says, 'deposed as local preacher in Southwark Vestry, December 1850, and expelled the Society for the same fault, March 1851'. But this could not keep the good man down. He continued to preach for the Reformers, and became their Editor and Book Steward. He was from the first an eager supporter of the Mutual Aid Association. He was one of the seventy at the historic meeting in Aldersgate on 18th July 1849 and was early given a place on the General Committee, of which he remained a member until 1893, two years before his death. From 1864 he was one of the editorial committee of the *Local Preachers' Magazine*, and for twenty-five years was responsible for the publishing and distribution of the journal. His pen was constantly employed in writing for the Magazine, but he used that implement to the most fruitful effect when *Grandfather Johnson* appeared in its pages. In addition to its wide circulation as a pamphlet, it was put into the form of a Service of Song, and this also proved a source of profit to the Association.

If Philip Parker's pen was indeed the means of bringing J. Wesley Walker into the Association's service, it did work of incalculable worth. As President, Trustee, and Editor of the Magazine, Wesley Walker served the Association with a wealth of gifts of mind and spirit, and will be for ever honoured among our 'great ones gone'. He had always dignity of presence and manner, but he possessed a ready and keen sense of humour. His reports of Aggregate Meetings in the Magazine are illumined by flashes from his racy and salty wit. The year of his presidency was the Diamond Jubilee of Queen Victoria's reign, and a loyal address was moved and approved in the Aggregate Meeting.

Place aux dames was again the order of the day when the brethren were awakened to the anomaly that women were on the plans as accredited local preachers but had hitherto not been admitted to the Association. It is strange that these elect ladies had submitted so long to this very ungallant and unbrotherly exclusion. But better late than never, and they were fully enfranchised when, in 1897, the Aggregate Meeting resolved that women local preachers 'shall be understood to be entitled to all rights and privileges in the Association which are enjoyed by men'. Even then one frightened male ejaculated: 'Does it mean they may come to the Aggregate Meeting?' And when that alarming prospect was confirmed, another gasped: 'Even taking appointments!' These timorous mortals might have been even more shocked if they could have foreseen the election of women to the General Committee, and even yet there are few who have dared to envisage the installation of a feminine President.

Arduous and exacting though the labours are of the Journal Secretary to the Aggregate Meeting, the office is not wreathed with enduring laurels, nor does its occupant often attain to historic fame. But at the Manchester Aggregate Meeting of 1898 the appointment was made of a brother who won for himself a unique place in the roll of scribes who have kept our records. C. Wesley Hall was a 'fellow of infinite jest, and most excellent fancy', who lightened the burden of his task by a spirit of unfailing cheerfulness, and who was the soul of faithfulness in all ways of service. Many a quip of his is still remembered; as, for instance, on the occasion of a proposal to increase the numbers of the General Committee, when he urged that room be found for some who were nearer the social status of the benefit members, and added drily that men were sometimes 'put on because they were better off'. Wesley Hall is one of the immortal 'characters' in our galaxy of notables.

William Ewart Gladstone died in 1898, and the Aggregate Meeting passed a resolution recording its appreciation of his lofty character, the magnificence of the example he had shown of the compatibility of the greatest saintliness with devoted national service in highest offices of state, and his transcendent gifts which were ever consecrated to the best interests of the people. This meeting was to have been favoured with a visit from the President of the Conference, Dr. W. L. Watkinson, but he was unable to fulfil his intention. He sent a letter, which was printed and distributed, in which he expressed his sympathy and goodwill toward the service of local preachers.

A sentence or two from this message from a prince of preachers may be quoted:

Your presence in our pulpits, bringing as it does, blessing to multitudes, is a standing protest against sacerdotalism, which from generation to generation threatens the simplicity that is in Christ. Your order is at once one of the greatest ministries of the Catholic Church, and one of the best defences of that Protestantism to which we owe so much. The separated pastorate of Methodism, together with its lay ministry, are binary stars, so evidently in the hands of Him who walks amid the golden candlesticks, that they reduce to absurdity the assumptions of ecclesiasticism.

The direct effect of your evangelical toil is simply incalculable. Through your instrumentality thousands of hamlets, villages, and towns, which would otherwise be painfully neglected, hear the saving truth. . . .

To a very large extent you lack those stimulating circumstances which aid the city pastor, and you rarely feel the electricity of a crowd. Still, in the truth you preach, and in the Master you serve, you find all needful inspiration; and, thank God, often when you pipe the dull place blossoms.

These poetic and eloquent expressions from so eminent a divine and 'master of assemblies' must have thrilled and impressed the laymen who heard the letter read, though the reporter rather tamely remarks only that it was 'received with applause'.

And so we come to 1899, the year of Jubilee. Birmingham, the venue of the first Aggregate Meeting proper in 1850, was appropriately the scene of the celebration of the Association's fiftieth year of life. It was scarcely to be expected that many of those present at the dawn of the creation of the Association would be spared to rejoice in its golden noontide, but one man was there whose heart must have been deeply moved as he remembered the days of old, the 'fightings without and fears within'. This was William Harris, who was Chairman of the foundation meetings in London, who was chosen as the first President, and who now, at the age of 86, was taking part once more in the annual meeting. Now all the conflicts were passed, the victory won, and it is good to know that this veteran warrior saw the triumph hour before he was called to his rest a year hence.

The election of John Barnsley as President for this exceptional year was an exceedingly happy choice. Meeting in Birmingham, thoughts naturally turned to a Birmingham man, and here was a prominent citizen, an active and devoted Methodist, one who as a preacher and an advocate of good causes was gifted above most with grace and power in speech. He did not have an unopposed return, for ex-President William Harris rose to nominate David Barr, but the voting left the result in no doubt; John Barnsley 325; David Barr 105.

The General Committee had been taking thought for the Jubilee, with the view of using the celebration to the best advantage. A programme had been outlined which aimed at securing an increase in the benefit membership, an additional 1,000 honorary members, and special services and meetings, with collections, in the Branches. The Aggregate Meeting instructed Branch secretaries and District conveners to arrange meetings to further this programme, the target for new honorary members being especially emphasized by Moses Atkinson.

A more immediate and tangible commemoration of the Golden Anniversary was the handing to the President of a cheque for £500 by Alderman W. H. Stephenson. He wished the money to be invested to found a fund to do for the widows what James Wild had done for the local preachers. The gift was accepted with grateful appreciation, and so stimulated the liberality of others that a lively financial 'love-feast' began later in the meeting. Contributions rolled in so swiftly and substantially that soon an additional sum of £550 was raised, making a grand total of one thousand guineas. The inception of the Jubilee Widows' fund was a noble inspiration. It provided sufficient means to give each widow a Christmas present of five shillings every year, and it is a more enduring memorial to the name of Stephenson than any 'storied urn' or monument of stone.

The widow annuitants benefited in another direction also from the expansive spirit generated by the Jubilee. Hitherto, their weekly allowance had been limited to 2*s*. 6*d*. It was now resolved to raise the maximum to 5*s*. A cautious and restrained generosity, one must admit, but prudence has ever been the governing virtue in the Association's administration. When men only were eligible for assistance, the maximum allowance was fixed at 4*s*. a week and remained so for years. Then it was raised to 5*s*. and in 1878 to 6*s*. In 1881, a motion to increase the maximum to 8*s*. was strongly opposed, the Honorary Secretary himself, being absent through illness, inditing a severe warning against 'a too lavish generosity on the part of impulsive brethren, who forget how soon the savings of years may be dissipated'. So a compromise was reached by an advance to only 7*s*.

But what gave rise
To no little surprise,
Nobody seemed one penny the worse!

Instead of savings disappearing, and financial stringency occurring, the 'lavish generosity' of an extra shilling a week was accompanied by an increase in subscriptions from the Methodist people. The fearful-hearted were rebuked, and in 1887 the bold step was taken of making a maximum of 8*s*.! It was not until nine years later in 1896, that the possible award was raised to 10*s*. This was the sum that Francis Pearson had hoped for in the beginning, but even now it was to be granted only 'in very extreme cases'. In this very year of Jubilee, three years after the allowance had been authorized, only two aged veterans were in receipt of such riches, and there had never been more than four or five, all of whom were nonagenarians, or thereabouts. No stigma of extravagance can be attached to the Association as almoners of the bounty entrusted to them to relieve the necessities of the saints.

The firm place in public esteem which the Association had won at this time is seen from the recognition its annual conferences received. At the Jubilee meeting, the Birmingham Free Church Council sent a distinguished deputation of welcome, including Mr. George Cadbury; the President of the Conference, the Rev. Hugh Price Hughes, sent a letter of greeting, regretting his unavoidable absence; and the Monday public meetting in Islington Wesleyan Church was presided over by Mr. R. W. Perks, M.P. It is also worthy of note that the Association was now attracting into its service the ablest and most influential local preachers in the Church. Not only were they eminent and active in Methodist circles, but many of them were to win rewards for valuable public services. A number of the brethren who were honoured later with the Royal accolade took part in the Jubilee gathering at Birmingham.

It is an impressive list: Sir John Barnsley, Sir William Smith, Sir John Bamford Slack, Sir Henry Lunn, Sir George Royle, Sir William H. Stephenson, Sir Thomas Rowbotham, Sir J. Tudor Walters, Sir Robert Perks. But while we gratefully 'praise famous men, men renowned for their power, giving counsel by their understanding', the Association's strong foundations are not in them, but in the quiet, faithful, constant labour of a numberless and nameless host who through the years have maintained the cause in village and town, in circuit and district, and have sought no other reward than the joy of seeing the loved work prosper in their hands.

To this great and glorious company of the valiant unknown be all the praise!

During its fifty years of activity, the Association had only two Treasurers, James Wild and John Carter, the latter still in office at the age of 88. Of the list of Trustees, Officers, and Committee in the Jubilee year, only one survives at this time of writing. His name appears as G. Royle, F.R.G.S., and he was to become President in 1908, and afterwards, for services to the nation in the first world war, Sir George Royle, C.B.E. Among the brethren appointed to take services on the Sunday appear the names of three who are happily still with us: Arthur Aykroyd, of Clapham, who was appointed in Walsall, William Edwards (then of Salford), who preached in Wellington, and is now our senior Trustee, and James Taylor, of Darlington, who went to Knighton, and who was for many years a valued member of the General Committee.

It may be appropriate to close this chapter with statements showing the income and expenditure of the Association at its Silver and Golden Jubilees. (Expenditure shown does not include general working expenses, which average about seven per cent. of the income.)

NUMBER OF MEMBERS

	Benefit	Honorary	Total
1874	1,840	530	2,370
1899	7,470	2,577	10,047

INCOME

Subscriptions, Collections, etc.	Dividends, etc	Total	Invested Funds
£	£	£	£
2,842	159	3,001	5,700
12,327	732	13,059	25,905

EXPENDITURE

	Sickness	Annuities	Deaths	Total
	£	£	£	£
1874	644	1,113	170	1,927
1899	2,974	7,134	782	10,890

TOTAL PAYMENTS from 1849

	Sickness	Annuities	Deaths	Total
	£	£	£	£
To 1874	17,222	20,187	9,210	46,619
To 1899	59,552	106,074	19,974	185,600

These are veritable 'tables of testimony', witnessing to the ever-widening stream of benevolence and blessing of which the Association was the channel, and revealing the ever-increasing favour of God and man toward its ministries of compassion. Its servants and friends pursued their way down the years 'in singleness of heart and aim,' giving themselves unselfishly and sacrificially to Christlike care of the poor and needy, seeking no other reward than the joy of doing good in the name and for the sake of the Lord of love, and, like wisdom, it was vindicated by its works. In 1851 the Rev. Samuel Jackson felt it his duty 'to point out some of those false steps which will eventually lead to its own destruction', and asked whether such an Association was worthy of countenance and support. Time has proved how foolish such insinuations were; and the generous love of the Methodist people, and the grateful thanks of the great host of those who have been comforted by its mission of mercy, are sufficient justification for this ministry to the saints in the past, and for continuing so to minister in the future.

CHAPTER SIX

UPWARD STILL, AND ONWARD

'WE HAVE not yet won the confidence of all good men, nor made manifest our works in every place, so as to silence the ignorance of those who speak evil of us falsely.' Such was the sorrowful confession made in the Annual Report of 1853. In less than fifty years all that had been changed. The Association had so grown in strength and stature that it marched into its second half-century with firm and confident step, assured of being known and approved as a work of God. Through days of precarious infancy and stormy adolescence, the good hand of the Lord was upon it, and it prospered in the thing for which it was raised up. Now, in the first year after its Jubilee, the retiring President, John Barnsley, can witness impressively to the way Methodism had taken the Association to its heart, and the Annual Report can speak of 'steady and continued progress', 'thus revealing yet again the fact, that as knowledge spreads, increased confidence is given, and consequently greater usefulness ensured'.

Brightly gleamed the path ahead, and the skies smiled above, serene and fair, so it appeared. Little did men guess, as they stood at the threshold of the new century, how near was the beginning of sorrows for the world they thought so safe. An age of wars and tumults was at hand, when 'nation shall rise against nation, and kingdom against kingdom'. It was the end of an era of security, and the dawn of the time of trembling and travail in the earth. Already things were coming to pass which troubled the peace of many hearts. The gathering clouds in South Africa had inspired a resolution, sponsored by Dr. Henry Lunn, in the 1899 Aggregate Meeting, praying for the preservation of peace, but war with the Boers had begun before the end of the year. It was the first step on the way to the world-shaking conflicts which have spread desolation in the earth. A year hence, Queen Victoria's long reign would close, and with her died Britain's last period of assured calm and complacent well-being. At home and abroad distressful days were ahead, with men's minds 'in perplexity for the roaring of the sea and the billows'.

But as yet these cataclysmic events were below the horizon, and the mutterings of the coming storm were audible only to those who had ears to hear. In June 1900 the Mutual Aid men met in Carver Street Chapel, Sheffield, in the highest spirits and in greater numbers than ever before. The Handbook gave the names of 577 delegates from a distance, and with the local brethren the attendance must have numbered nearly seven hundred. In the city and district 778 services were taken on the Sunday, 501 in Wesleyan chapels, 91 in the United Methodist Free Church, 109 in the Wesleyan Reform Union, and 77 in Methodist New Connexion churches. How great a contrast to the first Sheffield meeting in 1851! Sir William H. Stephenson was present, bearing the blushing honours of his recently conferred knighthood, and was the recipient of warm congratulations. But the rejoicings were not untouched by sorrow, for William Harris, the first President, Honorary Secretary in the Association's first year, and the first Editor, had died three days before the Aggregate Meeting began. His acceptance of a pastoral charge in South London in 1854 severed his official connection with the

Association, and his ministerial duties in various places in England and the Channel Islands occupied his attention for forty years, but in 1894, as has already been noted, he appeared and took part in the Aggregate Meeting in Burslem, dignified now by the style of the Rev. William Harris, D.D. The highest honour is due to him for the ability and ardour he displayed in the primal and creative years of the Association, and it is pleasing to remember that his affection for the beloved cause never changed through the years. He contributed to its funds, and when David Barr founded the Fillongley Cottage Homes for needy local preachers, William Harris gave a donation of £100, and became one of the Trustees. He died within a month of reaching the age of 87, but continued preaching to the last, taking two services on the last Sunday of his life.

Another grievous bereavement occurred in October of the same year, when M. L. Clapham, one of the Honorary Secretaries, died at the age of 62. He had held this important position since 1885. A man of quiet and modest disposition, he loved the Association with an intense affection and served it devotedly both as an official and an advocate. His place was not filled in the following year, the General Committee having decided that there was nothing for the second Secretary to do! It is open to question whether this odd opinion would be endorsed by the many 'juniors' who have shared this office. At any rate, Russell Johnson was accounted equal to carrying the burden without a colleague, and he was left alone in his glory.

It was not to be for long. Ere another Aggregate Meeting assembled, this gifted servant of the Association had been called to his reward. Increasing weakness of the heart overcame his powers of resistance, and on Easter Monday, 1902, his life and service here ended. Albert

Russell Johnson was first appointed as Honorary Secretary in 1881, he was elected President in 1884, and subsequently became one of the Trustees. Few men have laboured for the Association more devotedly and diligently than he. As counsellor and administrator he was sagacious and conscientious, and he was a man of many talents as a preacher, speaker, and writer. The Annual Reports written by him remain as testaments of his literary gifts. By the subscriptions of friends and fellow-workers, a brass plate, mounted on a marble block, was erected in Great Queen Street Chapel, of which he was a trustee and office-bearer. This was unveiled, a year after Russell Johnson's death, by William E. Skinner, the then President of the Association, and the Rev. James Chapman, Principal of Southlands College, delivered a memorial address. Russell Johnson was sometimes blunt, dogmatic, and impatient, but he was earnest, honest, and loyal to principle. A thorough Methodist, he abhorred Calvinism and sacerdotalism. He regarded the ministry of local preachers as a practical protest against the latter error, and he held the order to be the peculiar strength and glory of Methodism.

The successor to the portfolio of Honorary Secretary was found in John Bamford Slack, a man of brilliant parts, whose tenure of office was all too brief. He was the Liberal victor of a sensational by-election in the Mid-Herts division in the autumn of 1903, and in the following year felt compelled by the pressure of business to resign the Secretaryship. Among the other officers elected in 1902 was W. J. Back, who became one of the Auditors. Thus began an official career in the service of the Association which was to prove one of the most famous and effective in our annals, and was to crown the name of William James Back with the unfading laurels of a great and heroic leader.

The meeting in 1902 was marked by another deed of generosity on the part of Sir William Stephenson. It was found that the income of his Jubilee Widows Fund was not sufficient to give every widow beneficiary a Christmas gift of five shillings. Sir William therefore offered to supplement the capital by a further £500, if the Association would raise the sum of £300 before the end of the year. The challenge was accepted, subscriptions amounting to £331 were received within the stated time, and the widows were assured of their Christmastide bounty for some years to come. Another interesting addition to the general funds of the Association was reported this year in the form of a legacy of over £2,500 from an Anglican clergyman, the Rev. B. Deakin, of Worcester. He had been converted in his youth under the preaching of a Methodist local preacher, and in helping in this way the brotherhood to which the unknown evangelist belonged Mr. Deakin found a lovely way of expressing his grateful remembrance.

Up to this date Presidents had been elected and inducted into office in the same meeting. How many aspiring and optimistic brethren had come prepared with presidential addresses in hope of being called up higher, and had departed with their great words unspoken, who can tell? So many advantages appertained to an interval between designation and inauguration that it is not surprising that at long last it was decided that the Aggregate Meeting should elect the President a year in advance. As with all changes for the better, the wonder is that this good custom had to wait until 1902 for its coming.

The last days of the dying year were overcast by the shadow of a great sorrow in Mutual Aid circles. On Christmas Eve that great servant of God and of the Association, Samuel Danks Waddy, finished his course on earth at the age of 72. It has been claimed for him that the turning point in the Association's fortunes dates from the time when he gave it his allegiance and became its President. Prior to 1870, the mists of suspicion clouded the judgement of many regarding this novel laymen's organization, and progress was slow and fluctuating. But the adherence and advocacy of so eminent and eloquent a Methodist as S. D. Waddy wrought a swift and decided change. A movement approved by one of such distinguished and unquestionable ancestry and attainments could not be anything but good and worthy, and seeing such a man supporting it, 'they could say nothing against it'. The eldest son of Dr. Waddy, a President of Conference and Governorof Wesley College, Sheffield, he became a leading barrister and Queen's Counsel, entered Parliament as Liberal member for Edinburgh, and was subsequently appointed Recorder of Sheffield and a County Court Judge. In addition to his Presidency, Judge Waddy served the Association as a Trustee, and was ever ready to speak in its interests. 'One of the greatest preachers of his time, there has been no greater lay preacher in the Methodist Churches', was the testimony borne to him when he died. Be that as it may, it is undoubted that to Samuel D. Waddy the Association owed much of its increasing favour with the people called Methodists, and his name will be ever numbered and honoured among the most illustrious of our greatest and best. His son, Samuel Garbutt Waddy, also lived to serve the Association with devotion and distinction. He was much beloved for his personal graces and gifts, which were recognized by his election as a Trustee, and he would have been raised to the highest place as President had it not been for his deafness in the latter years.

Irrefutable evidence of the steady progress and

growing stability of the Association was afforded in the Report for the year ended 31st March 1903. The income exceeded £20,000 for the first time; honorary members passed the figure of 3,000 for the first time; the membership had risen to 11,812 in 565 branches; the number of annuitants, 647, was the largest ever reported (421 local preachers and 226 widows); and the total payments for annuities, sickness, and deaths amounted to £14,735, the average weekly allowances to men being 7*s.* and to widows 4*s.* Pressing on with singleness of purpose, turning not from it to the right hand or to the left, these servants of the compassionate Christ had made their way prosperous, and they were granted good success.

The next year brought a number of changes in the executive, which were to prove pregnant with boundless benefit and blessing to the Association, heralding, if it had been known, its brightest days. To succeed J. Bamford Slack, whose duties 'in another place' deprived the Association of his official services, W. E. Skinner and W. J. Back were elected as Honorary Secretaries. The Annual Reports of the former, combining as was wittily said, 'the archaeological and historical, the statistical and the analytical, the hortatory, prophetical, and oratorical', were to become a notable feature of the Association's account of its stewardship for many years; while the promotion of the latter raised to a position of highest authority and influence one who made the Association the ruling passion of his great heart, and served it with the sacrificial devotion of his life.

The appointment of William Edwards to the vacant post of Auditor marked the beginning of an official connection which was to continue for more than forty years, and introduced into the executive council of the Association a brother whose knowledge, wisdom, and statesmanship have been of incalculable service, and have been freely and unstintedly given. In the same year, J. Wesley Walker, who had been co-Editor of the Magazine with the Rev. I. E. Page since 1895, felt obliged on account of public and other duties to relinquish his position. He had done outstanding service in this capacity, charm, humour, and spiritual grace characterizing all he wrote. James Kerry, of Highbury, was elected to share the editorial chair.

In 1907, John Carter, who had succeeded James Wild as Treasurei in 1866, was 96 years old. He was still able to sign documents as a Trustee, but it was not unnaturally thought that the time had come for the appointment of a younger Treasurer. The lot fell on Charles Heap, of Rochdale, who had been President in 1896. Such was the affection felt for John Carter that his name continued to be printed in the list of officers as Past Honorary Treasurer until his death on 31st December 1908 at the age of 97, a distinctive honour accorded to no other in the history of the Association.

The year 1907 was made memorable by a further enlargement of the constituency from which members of the Association might be drawn. The Bible Christian Church was in process of uniting with the Methodist New Connexion and the United Methodist Free Churches, and the question of making the Bible Christian local preachers eligible for membership was the subject of fraternal negotiations. It was ultimately agreed that, on payment by the Bible Christian Church of the sum of £3,000, their local preachers should be allowed to enter the Mutual Aid Association on the terms laid down in the Rules, and that the fifteen brethren already receiving assistance from the Benevolent Fund of that Church should have their allowances maintained without entrance fee or subscription. On

2nd August 1907 the last Conference of the Bible Christian Church confirmed the provisional agreement, and on 12th October a cheque for the amount named (with a little interest due to the delay in payment) was received. By the following May it was estimated that nearly three hundred local preachers from the newly admitted section had become members of the Association.

Professor G. M. Trevelyan, in his *English Social History*, writes of the 1830's that 'the sentiment of humanity was now a great force in politics'. The Anti-Slavery and Factory Acts may be regarded as evidence in support of this dictum. But as yet there was no urgent and widespread concern in Church or State for the improvement of the general social conditions of the people. The lot of the poor and the workless, and the friendless old, was not a happy one in the first half of the nineteenth century, despite the various works of charity and philanthropy which piety felt it its duty to perform. For the mass of unfortunates, the untender mercies of the Poor Law were their only hope. 'So many hundred thousands sit in the workhouses (pleasantly so-named, because work cannot be done in them); and other hundred thousands have not yet got even workhouses.' No wonder Thomas Carlyle fulminated with all his wealth of invective against the 'scenes of woe and destitution and desolation' to be found in our cities and towns. But as knowledge of these evils spread, and public opinion gained wider power and opportunity to express itself in municipalities and Parliament, the demand for the State to devise measures for social betterment grew more and more insistent. It was felt as a blot on the nation's escutcheon that citizens when disabled and infirm and old should be left to seek a refuge within the dreaded portals of pauperdom. So when the Liberal

Government produced its Old Age Pensions Bill in 1908 all save the incorrigible individualists, who prophesied the decay of the virtues of thrift and self-reliance, hailed the measure as a deed of political justice and social righteousness. Voluntary philanthropic societies welcomed the new proposals as eagerly as anybody, but naturally they were compelled to consider the effect of them on their own special work. Among these institutions the Mutual Aid Association was bound to be affected. It is to the lasting credit of the responsible officers at that time that they took a reasoned and statesmanlike view of the position. They welcomed the beginnings of State provision for aged and worn-out workers, which was cognate to the service of the Association. So far from lessening the need of such service, they envisaged this national assistance to the over-seventies as an opportunity for increasing the Association's grants to the younger brethren and widows, and the consequent necessity for increasing its income for benevolent purposes. All the branch secretaries and annuitants were circularized, and where necessary the Association's allowances were reduced in order that the full amount of the national pension might be claimed. It has never been the policy of the Association to relieve the State of its bounden duty to its citizens. The first effect of the Old Age Pensions Act, which came into operation on 1st January 1909, was a reduction of nearly £1,000 in the amount expended on annuities, but this saving was only a temporary phase. Larger grants to the younger brethren and sisters, and the steady increase in the numbers of annuitants, soon caused the expenditure to rise again, proving that this voluntary ministry to the poor and needy was as necessary as ever. It was evident to all who have eyes to see that no State machinery can wholly mitigate the tragedies of age and affliction, and when legislation has done its utmost there will still be a need for the kindly hand of human love and mercy to be stretched out to heal and help. Sad indeed would it be if the bereft and burdened saints of the household of faith had none to care for them but the minions of a Public Assistance system. Voluntary service can never cease to be of supreme value in the fields of human endeavour, and it must always be of especial worth and merit in the ministries of the Christian Church, be they spiritual or social. For this cause, such Christ-inspired fellowships of service as the Mutual Aid Association will ever have a place in the economy of a living Church.

When, in 1910, the Association held its annual meeting for the third time in Newcastle-on-Tyne, Sir William Stephenson, attired in his robes as Lord Mayor of the city, came to the platform to offer a civic welcome. This was the fourth time Sir William had occupied the office of Chief Magistrate, and on the two previous occasions of the Aggregate Meeting's visit he had been elected as President. Twenty-seven years before, the delegates numbered only 128, the membership was just over 4,000, the income was £4,400, and there were 207 annuitants, receiving £2,157 (an average of 2*s.* 7½*d.* a week). Now the income had grown to £20,000, the membership to 13,479, the annuitants totalled 789, with grants amounting to £10,744 (averaging 6*s.* 0½*d.* a week for men and 4*s.* 3*d.* for widows). Truly might the chronicler introduce his record of the proceedings with the exulting words: 'On they go from strength to strength.'

In March 1910 David Barr died at the age of 79. He had been President in 1906, but he will be best remembered for his instrumentality in the erection of a group of cottages for aged local preachers at Fillongley, the village of his birth. In the following year, a mural brass tablet was unveiled in Ripley Wesleyan Church by Miss Agnes Slack, in memory of her brother, Sir John Bamford Slack. Sir John had died in February 1909 at the early age of 51. He had served Methodism and the Association with devoted zeal, and his brilliant gifts were entirely consecrated to the service of the highest and best things. His country and his Church lost a noble son when he was cut off in the zenith of his powers.

The introduction of the Liberal Government's National Health Insurance Bill in 1911 confronted the Association with perhaps the most critical moment in its history. The fluttering of its dovecotes caused by the Old Age Pensions Act was a mild susurration compared with the gusts of feeling and apprehension stirred by the far-reaching provisions of this new adventure in social legislation. Many will recall the fury and ferocity with which the Bill, and its sponsor, Mr. Lloyd George, were attacked by those who detested this advance in welfare service by the State. There was no trace of this violent opposition in Mutual Aid circles, but there was concern and bewilderment about the effect of the Bill on the position and activities of the Association. As with the Pensions Act, how could these Christian men do other than welcome the Government's awakening to the duty of caring for people in distress? They had been doing this themselves for so long that they could not but rejoice in the benefits now to be provided by the State. Richard Lindley, who had become co-Editor of the Magazine (the Rev. I. E. Page now acting as consulting Editor) expressed the sentiments of all when he wrote:

> Social reform has received one of the greatest lifts that this century has known. For the first time in history the Government of our country is proposing to take charge of its sick and invalid citizens. Surely this is a result of the teaching of the Gospel of Him whose compassion was great toward the multitude, and who went about curing the sick.

It is work we, as a Mutual Aid Association, have been doing for our members during the last sixty years. And as in Old Age Pensions, so in this, we claim to have led the way.

But the question for us now is: How will this Bill, if it becomes an Act, affect us? Does it mean that our work as a sick society is done, or shall we become an Approved Society, and place ourselves under the ruling of the Act?

Yes, that indeed was the question, and a tricky and thorny one it was to answer. A great debate took place in the June Aggregate Meeting at Bolton, revealing a deep difference of opinion between some of the finest and most expert minds. Time was too short, and the matter too momentous, to permit of a final decision then, so it was agreed to appoint a sub-committee to watch the progress of the Bill, and to adjourn the Aggregate *sine die*, and to call it together again specially to consider what the future policy was to be. Upon one thing, above all, everyone was agreed. No member of the brotherhood would be allowed to suffer loss, and the benevolent work of the Association must be carried on.

The Insurance Bill, 'through rude and stormy scenes', at last was placed on the Statute Book, and the Association had to face the consequences. Every step was taken with full awareness of its seriousness, and after keen and free discussion. First, the General Committee held a special meeting on 18th January 1912, at Central Buildings, Westminster, to which the offices of the Association had been transferred in the previous June. The Honorary Secretaries proposed a recommendation to the adjourned Aggregate Meeting that an Approved Society be not formed. An amendment was moved by A. J. Cash that an Approved Society be formed at once. A debate lasting nearly three hours ensued, and ultimately the amendment was lost by 19 votes to 9, with one neutral. A sub-committee was appointed to draw up appropriate resolutions, and the adjourned

Aggregate Meeting was fixed for Saturday 9th March.

On 17th February the General Committee met in Liverpool, when the resolutions of the sub-committee were presented and discussed at length. Most of them were adopted unanimously, and no substantial opposition to any was encountered. The main resolutions to be submitted for the approval of the Aggregate Meeting were as follows:

This Aggregate Meeting decides not to become an Approved Society, or to form an Approved Society, as a section of the Association, under the National Insurance Act, 1911.

From this date, no new benefit members, under the conditions hitherto obtaining, shall be accepted.

All benefit members may continue their membership in the Association at the present rate of subscription and scale of benefits, subject to the right of the Association, under its Rules, to make any alterations either in the rate of subscription or scale of benefits that may be found necessary.

The basis of membership of the Association shall be:

(*a*) Honorary members (as at present) who shall pay one guinea, or upwards, per annum.
(*b*) Benefit members who continue in membership in accordance with the above resolution.
(*c*) Members retained for restricted benefits.
(*d*) New members, being local preachers, to be admitted on an annual subscription of

The organisation of the Association shall continue on its present lines, as far as practicable.

The amount of the subscription to be paid by members retained, and by new members, was referred to a sub-committee consisting of the Honorary and General Secretaries and the Auditors. Their recommendations, which were reported to the General Committee at Sheffield on 8th March, were as follows:

Annual subscription for brethren retained for a limited membership, 3*s.*; for brethren joining under 45 years of age, 3*s.*; for brethren over 45 and under 55 years, 4*s.*; for brethren over 55 years, 5*s.* These proposals were approved by a large majority.

On the morrow, Saturday 9th March, the fateful Aggregate Meeting extraordinary assembled in Carver Street Chapel. The debate was opened by the Honorary Secretary, W. J. Back, who moved the adoption of the General Committee's recommendation that an Approved Society be not formed. It was perhaps the greatest moment in his career, and his qualities of vision and leadership were never more clearly manifested. He emphasized the difficult and complex nature of the crisis that faced them, and declared that the whole future of the Association depended on the issue of that day. He pointed out the complications in administration which would be caused by Government control and oversight, and the competition which would be bound to occur with other Approved Societies. The Association's benevolent work, the voluntary advocacy of the brethren, and the freewill giving of the Methodist people, would all be seriously affected if a State-regulated Society were set up. The resolution was seconded by Edwin Talbot, chairman of the Higher Education Committee of the West Riding.

An amendment expressing the opposite view was proposed by A. J. Cash, and seconded by William Edwards, the Honorary Auditor, whose experience in the insurance world lent weight to his words. He regarded the actuarial position of the Association as far from satisfactory, and saw in this new Act an opportunity of putting it on a sound basis. His skilful pleading had a marked effect, but when George Royle rose to reply to what he called these 'dangerous fallacies', the impression soon began to fade. 'We have never done our work on professed business lines', he declared, and urged that the Association should maintain its purely benevolent calling and character. Much speaking followed, one member quoting the opinion of Arthur Henderson that the widening breach between the Churches and labour would be made wider still by the Association becoming an Approved Society! This wild surmise probably frightened nobody, but it was soon apparent on which side the weight of argument was falling. When the amendment was put, it was lost by a large majority, and the Committee's resolution was then carried by an overwhelming vote. The passage of time has proved the wisdom of this decision. The genius and spirit of the Association were preserved, and its beneficent operations have continued with ever-extending range and benediction. All the benefit members were advised by letter of the new conditions, and out of 6,000 replies received, only 200 intimated their desire to leave the Association. So ended one of the most critical periods in the history of this great society. Division of opinion there was, but no diversity of purpose. Brotherly love prevailed over all, and the fellowship of hearts and minds remained unbroken as it was in the beginning, is now, and, please God, ever shall be.

CHAPTER SEVEN

THROUGH CLOUD AND SUNSHINE

BRIGHT and fair were the days of June when the annual meetings were held in Sheffield in 1914. No tremor of the convulsions that were soon to shake the world disturbed those peaceful hours. In sweet and happy fellowship the brethren met to rejoice, with thankful hearts, in the continued good success of the work they loved. Less than two months later the country was at war with a fierce and mighty foe, and terror and tragedy and tears were to blot out the sunshine of life in countless hearts and homes for more than four years.

The possible effect of such a national calamity on religious and charitable organizations gave the responsible authorities much cause for apprehension, and the leaders of the Association were not exempt from the general anxiety. It was immediately decided that the membership of brethren who had joined the forces should be safeguarded during their service with the remission, at its close, of any arrears of subscription, if necessary. But the fears of a largely diminished income proved baseless, and in spite of numerous appeals for a variety of war charities, the revenue of the Association remained remarkably constant, and the receipts from collections were actually increased. In districts and branches, officials and members stuck manfully to their tasks, and the Methodist people supported them with open-handed generosity.

But 1914 was not only a year of gloom and grief for

Sir William H. Stephenson, D.L., J.P., D.C.L.

President 1883 and 1895

the nation; it cast the shadow of sorrow over the household of the Association. On 20th May, John Harding, the beloved General Secretary, died. For thirty-one years he had served the Association in that pivotal position, with undivided and undeviating loyalty, and had won for himself the affection and trust of the whole brotherhood, A man of kindly and gentle disposition, of stainless Christian character, competent in business, faithful and patient in the discharge of duty, and loved by all, John Harding was deeply mourned, and his passing was felt as a grievous personal loss by all his fellow-workers. As a tribute from friends and colleagues, a marble cross was erected over his grave in Acton cemetery, and a stained-glass window placed in Brixton Hill chapel, where John Harding worshipped for many years, the window being unveiled by the President, W. J. Back.

At its meeting in July of the same year, the General Committee interviewed six candidates for the General Secretaryship who had been selected by a sub-committee from more than one hundred and thirty applications. The voting in the first ballot showed a majority for W. E. Noddings, and on his name being then put to the meeting, his election was heartily and unanimously approved. It was a happy day that fixed this choice of a new Secretary, and a providentially-guided choice it was to prove. Coming to his new office, at the age of 34, from a responsible position in the Seaton Carew Ironworks Company, Durham, William E. Noddings entered upon a career of service for the Association which was marked throughout by efficiency and fidelity and selfless devotion. Always so much more than an official, his brotherliness, his integrity, his kindly shrewdness, and his spiritual intensity won the high regard of everyone. When he took up his appointment an editorial note in the Magazine: ran 'It is something to live in the esteem and affection of the brethren throughout the land, and this is the reward that awaits Bro. Noddings, if he succeeds, as we devoutly expect and pray, in the big task now committed to his care.' If he succeeds! A needless and most unvirtuous 'if'. When W. E. Noddings retired on 31st December 1946, after more than thirty-two years' honourable service, the tributes paid to him at Headquarters, and from all quarters, demonstrated beyond all question that he had nobly won the reward of his brethren's esteem and affection, which, next to his Lord's 'Well done' is the best thanks any man can receive for his life's work.

The war dragged its slow length along, bringing loss and sorrow widespread and immeasurable, but through it all the Association's ministries of benevolence and comfort never failed. Nor was there any decline in the generous sympathy of Methodist friends in support of this compassionate service. In 1918, the last year of the tragic conflict, collections in the churches increased by nearly £2,000, and free subscriptions and donations (the latter including a gift of £1,000 from Mr. Joseph Rank) by almost a like sum. The total income from the branches was £21,576, a net increase of £3,866, while the expenditure on annuities, sickness, etc., had mounted to £15,422. The rising costs of living due to the war were now pressing hardly on everyone, and the kindly hearts of the Mutual Aid officers began to be concerned about the unhappy lot of their needy annuitants. The Rules permitted grants 'not exceeding ten shillings' for local preachers, and 'not exceeding five shillings' for widows. In 1917 the Aggregate Meeting approved the raising of these maximum allowances to 12*s.* and 6*s.* respectively. Even so, the average allowances reported in 1918 were only 6*s.* 1¾*d.* for men and 4*s.* 5*d.* for widows.

At Nottingham, in 1919, the Honorary Secretary proposed the exclusion of the limiting words, thus making possible grants in excess of the amounts stated. This was passed by the Aggregate Meeting, but, canny and cautious as ever, with the stipulation that all excess grants 'shall be for one year only, and shall be subject to revision when the maximum grants are fixed at the Aggregate Meeting of 1920'. With the passing of the months, a bolder and more liberal spirit prevailed; and when at Darlington in the following year W. J. Back, the Honorary Secretary, moved to amend the Rules so as to eliminate the restrictions on allowances, and to give the General Committee unfettered discretion, the resolution was carried without hesitation and with complete unanimity. It was a happy and sensible sanction to bestow. The powers then conferred on the Committee have made possible larger bounties in needful cases, and at no time have the traditional standards of prudence and economy in administration been disregarded.

In 1921 the cloud of another heavy bereavement hung darkly over the fellowship of the Association. At Wimbledon, on 9th April, the senior Honorary Secretary, William E. Skinner, read his draft Annual Report to the General Committee, and received the thanks and congratulations of his brethren. On the 20th of the same month an operation became necessary, and on the 22nd he passed away. It was a severe loss, for he was a great servant of the Association. Elected to the General Committee in 1888, he was soon after appointed an Honorary Auditor, and in 1902 was raised to highest honour as President. Two years later, on Sir J. Bamford Slack's resignation, he was chosen to be Honorary Secretary, with W. J. Back as his junior colleague. For seventeen years the task of writing the Annual Reports was both his duty and his delight, and his careful, lucid, and polished paragraphs transformed a statement of facts and figures into a literary exercise of high excellence. At first a schoolmaster, he afterwards became sub-editor of the *Methodist Recorder*. In Stoke Newington, Tottenham, Forest Gate, and Stratford, he filled many circuit offices, and was a local preacher of great acceptance. A sterling, conscientious, devout man, W. E. Skinner left an abiding influence. Precise, punctilious, a little pompous perhaps, he was not exactly an easy man to know, but he was faithful in all things, mature in judgement, and he served the Association with wholehearted zeal and unswerving loyalty. Loving friends joined together to provide a large framed photograph of their departed colleague, and this was received in the name of the Association by the President, William Douthwaite, at a moving little ceremony in the Head Office, where the portrait hangs as a permanent memorial. A beautiful marble cross was also placed on his grave in Ilford cemetery.

Another notable figure passed from the fellowship below in the same month of April. Benjamin Gough Berry, who had been President in 1907, was born and bred in Kent, and his burly frame and beaming countenance were a testimonial to the salubrity and freshness of the Kentish air, and the healthful property of its orchards and uplands. He was a great lover of the fellowship of the Mutual Aid, and was one of the most ardent of its advocates.

OUR ROYAL PATRONS

But though the passing years brought their shadows and sorrows, they brought cheer and sunshine too. One of the happiest events in our history has now to be recorded. In the February 1922 issue of the *Local Preachers' Magazine*, this note appeared: 'Every member of the Association will hear with the greatest pleasure that the President has received from His Majesty the King and Her Majesty the Queen Their gracious consent to give Their patronage to the Wesleyan Methodist Local Preachers Mutual Aid Association. Their Majesties have each caused a cheque for ten guineas to be sent as a contribution to our funds.' Further particulars were promised in the next number of the Magazine.

In March the Magazine printed the following letters, which had been forwarded by the President for publication:

YORK COTTAGE,
SANDRINGHAM,
NORFOLK.
18*th January*, 1922

DEAR SIR,

I am commanded to inform you that the King and Queen will be pleased to become patrons of the Wesleyan Methodist Local Preachers Mutual Aid Association, and in that capacity Their Majesties will give a donation of Ten Guineas.

Sir Edward Wallington, the Treasurer to the Queen, will communicate with you with regard to Her Majesty's donation.

Yours faithfully,
(*Signed*) FREDERICK PONSONBY,
Keeper of the Privy Purse.

To W. DOUTHWAITE, ESQ.

BUCKINGHAM PALACE.
13*th January*, 1922

DEAR SIR,

With reference to your letter of the 17th November last, addressed to His Majesty King George, I am commanded to say that the Queen will be pleased to accord her patronage to the Wesleyan Methodist Local Preachers Mutual Aid Association, and to give a donation of Ten Guineas in compliance with your request.

I beg to enclose cheque for £10 10*s*.

I am, Dear Sir,
Yours faithfully,
(*Signed*) EDWARD WALLINGTON.

To W. DOUTHWAITE, ESQ.

King George the Fifth, most gracious of Sovereigns,

and beloved by all his subjects, has passed away, leaving the fragrant memory of a great King and a good man. Queen Mary is happily still with us, equally beloved for her graciousness and goodness, and for the example of her life of devoted service. The history of Their Majesties' kindness to the Mutual Aid Association owes much to William Douthwaite, who was President in 1921, and to him we are indebted for such details as may be published.

It began in 1914, before the outbreak of the Great War, when King George and Queen Mary were visiting the new headquarters of the Y.M.C.A., in Tottenham Court Road, London. The Royal party was conducted by Lord Kinnaird, and when a halt was made near to where Douthwaite was standing, the Queen remarked that he looked so healthy that he evidently must have been well mothered. 'By one of the poorest, but most loyal of your subjects, your Majesty', he replied.

Later in the year, when the war had broken out, the first batch of Canadian soldiers arrived in this country and were billeted in Windsor Great Park. The Y.M.C.A. quickly got to work in their interests, and members of the Royal household and neighbouring gentlefolk assisted in looking after the men. Among the other helpers was William Douthwaite. A religious service was arranged for each Sunday evening, and these were conducted on alternate Sundays by Archdeacon Sinclair, of London, and William Douthwaite. One very wet night, when the latter was the speaker, there were so many officers and men outside wanting to get in, that he went to the platform and asked if more room could be made. Immediately, those who were sitting rose and piled up their chairs, the room was swiftly packed, and the audience stood for the whole of the service. One of the Princesses, who had been playing the piano for the singing, asked Douthwaite at the close if he was a clergyman. He explained that he was a Methodist local preacher, one of the thousands who voluntarily gave their services in towns, villages, and hamlets all over England. 'It is so good and wonderful', was her comment.

The memory of the interest shown in high places in his work was cherished in William Douthwaite's heart, and when he came to the Presidency in 1921, he began to ponder the possibility of making Their Majesties acquainted with the constitution and aims of the Mutual Aid Association. At last he decided to write and give an account of the work, telling how it was supported by collections in the churches and by the subscriptions of life and honorary members, and how valuable to the country was the faithful witness of this body of voluntary evangelists. Happening to meet Mr. Edward Shortt, the then Home Secretary, who was an old friend, he secured the promise of his assistance in the matter. Almost immediately, replies were received from both King George and Queen Mary, through the official channels, each enclosing ten guineas as a life member's subscription, and each spontaneously and graciously extending their patronage to the Association.

Needless to say, these manifestations of Their Majesties' sympathy with and interest in our great benevolent work were received with the profoundest gratitude. The Royal bounty was an added inspiration to every officer and member, and a message of good cheer to all our aged, sick, and needy brothers and sisters. From many a heart, and from many a family altar, prayer ascended to the King of kings that the Divine blessing might be abundantly bestowed on Their Majesties and the Royal House. And perhaps the grateful prayers of the poor, who found in them a help in need, were the thanks Their Majesties valued most.

The General Committee duly recorded its official appreciation of the favour shown by our Royal patrons, and directed that a letter of grateful acknowledgement should be sent. Sincere thanks were also accorded to the President for his service in connection with this happy event. The Association's letter is given below:

To THEIR MAJESTIES THE KING AND QUEEN.

YOUR MAJESTIES,

Your letters sent to the President of this Association, dated January 13th and 18th last, have been received with great pleasure and satisfaction by the General Committee, meeting in Liverpool, February 18th, 1922. Your gracious consent to accord your patronage to our work, and to become Life Members, has not only given much joy to the Methodist Churches of our land, but we as an Association feel specially favoured in the great honour you have conferred upon us. Such recognition will be a great inspiration to our cause, for, as already intimated to you, we are not only loyal and devoted sons of the Empire, but we stand for a beautiful ministry of benevolence, and for the proclamation of those spiritual truths which help to build up personal character, and which constitute the strength and stability of any Nation or Empire.

We are, on behalf of the General Committee,

Yours obediently,

(*Signed*) WM. DOUTHWAITE,
President.

(*Signed* WM. JAS. BACK,
Hon. Secretary.

Thus ends the story of what was said, written, and done at that time, but the influence of the good deed done by our gracious Patrons has never ended. It quickened, and still quickens, the interest of friends beyond our borders, and it gave a fillip and a finer edge to the zeal of every official and member. We had much reason to be thankful for the Royal favour then, and we continue to have. To Queen Mary, for whose long life we give God thanks, a message of loyal and affectionate greeting and remembrance is sent every year from the Aggregate Meeting, and her kind reply is greatly appreciated. It was a cause of much gratification and encouragement when the message was received that it was the pleasure of King George the Sixth to continue the patronage which his Father had granted us. The Association is a brotherhood of men and women who delight to obey the apostolic injunction: 'Fear God; honour the King.' At the first Aggregate Meeting proper in 1850, Francis Pearson said he knew of no class of men in the Kingdom more attached to the Queen and Constitution, or who had rendered more essential service to the State, than the body of Methodist local preachers. The influence which they, as a body, exerted upon society at large was as powerful as that of any of the clergy. They entered the towns, villages, and scattered hamlets throughout the land, and taught men to read their Bibles and to pray, that so they might be better fitted for this life as well as for that which is to come. In their efforts, they came fairly in contact with the masses of society, and he believed they had, by the blessing of God, raised the morals of the people, taught them to keep the laws, to respect the rights of their fellow-men, and in every proper and legitimate manner to uphold the Constitution under which they had the privilege to live. Pearson concluded his laudatory estimation of the brotherhood by suggesting that they, as a body, ought to express their loyalty to the Queen's person, and their attachment to the Constitution of which she was the head. He then moved 'that a loyal and Christian address be drawn up by the General Committee, and in due course presented to the Queen.' This proposition was carried with loud applause by the standing vote of the Aggregate Meeting. As it was at the first, so it has been through the years. In the name of the

Association, loyal addresses have been sent on State occasions, such as Queen Victoria's Golden and Diamond Jubilees, on the deaths of monarchs, and on the accession of their successors. This was done as in duty bound, expecting nothing again. Thus, the spontaneous and unsolicited bestowal of the Royal patronage came as an immense and immeasurable enheartenment, and it remains so to this day.

The Bristol Aggregate Meeting of 1922 was memorable for many things. The Annual Report was the first to be written by W. J. Back, and he had an inspiring statement to make. The membership was increased by 1,210 and now numbered 15,909; honorary members had subscribed £6,110, an increase of £2,259; and collections totalled £15,513, which was an advance of £3,869. The sum of £3,834 was paid out for sickness, an increase of £1,139; and benevolent allowances amounted to £11,644, an increase of £5,062. There were 718 annuitants, twelve of whom were over 90 years of age. Nor was our primary work as preachers forgotten. 'The Association has always stood for evangelism, as well as benevolence. Our members are preachers first, and pleaders for money next.' It is good to know that this note has always been dominant in the Association's career.

The President for the year was Arthur Cowling, and his inaugural address was one of the finest in our history. Its vision, passion, range of thought and understanding of the times, roused his audience to enthusiasm. It was a lofty utterance, and the emotional force of the speaker left an impression which has remained a vivid memory in the minds of all who heard it.

Owing to illness, Charles Heap had been compelled to resign the position of Honorary Treasurer, and John

Pritchard Williams, of Ealing, was elected in his stead. Charles Heap had been President in 1896, and became the Treasurer in 1908. He died in a little more than a year after laying down his office, leaving the memory of a saintly character and a generous spirit.

When Theodore Roosevelt left the White House, Mr. Dooley remarked that the last thing anyone could call him would be a 'retiring' President. William Douthwaite might have had a better claim to the adjective in some sense, but not in all. For having just resigned the crown of the Presidency, he was at once called to share the office of Honorary Secretary, and willingly consented to undertake the task. But he was not able to carry the burden long, and in November he resigned the post. For some time W. J. Back had been handicapped in his service by illness and pain. He had gallantly borne the load of responsibility which his office of Honorary Secretary laid on his shoulders, and his great heart never failed to inspire him to give his utmost of strength to the service of the cause which he loved so dearly. But in 1924 the necessity of having a colleague became urgent, and he proposed that Arthur Cowling should be appointed. The ex-President had established himself so deeply and firmly in the affection and esteem of his brethren that his election was carried with acclaim. Never was a more timely and fortunate appointment made, for less than two years later, owing to his beloved senior's breakdown, the chief executive position in the Association fell to his charge. How nobly he played his part all who knew him remember well and are proud to tell.

The year 1924 was notable as a 'milestone' year, for in it was commemorated the seventy-fifth anniversary of the Association's foundation. Three-quarters of a century had passed, and the success and progress of this fellowship of love and service had been beyond all hope and thought. The bare figures speak more eloquently than any words. In the first year 1,260 members joined; now there were 17,012. The number of annuitants was thirty-two; now it was 847; weekly allowances were limited then to 2*s.* 6*d.*; that restriction had gone, and cases of proved need were receiving as much as 24*s.* The amount expended in annuities had risen from £57 12*s.* in the first year to £20,917 in 1923. Honorary members, who then numbered under fifty, had risen to 7,393. Collections and donations had totalled £59 18*s.* In this latest year, collections had amounted to £14,691, and donations to £2,486. In the first year £1,060 was invested; the investments now stood at £80,529. It is a record of which the Mutual Aid men might be pardonably proud. But in all things they gave God the glory, and remembered that it was He who had brought them out into 'a large place'. Marvellous in their eyes indeed it was, but they knew it was the Lord's doing. The Report presented in the seventy-fifth year closed with these words: 'We would again emphasize our constant dependence upon the Holy Spirit, we have been conscious in a very wonderful way of His presence with us, and we are filled with humble gratitude.' In that sense of dependence on God's presence and blessing the Association began its work, and the assurance of His favour has been its stimulus and encouragement all the way along.

CHAPTER EIGHT

THE YEARS OF HARVEST

IT WAS NOW plain beyond the shadow of doubt, and beyond any envious critic's power to deny, that the Mutual Aid Association was a house well builded on a foundation firm and deep. Changes there might be, and would be, in its ordering and its ways of service, but its place in the love and sympathies of the Methodist people was assured from this time forth. Tempests had beaten and torrents had burst against this house, but it had withstood them all, a monument to the faith and vision, the fortitude and the self-denying consecration, of laymen from all walks of life. Always independent of Conference connection and direction, the work had been carried on from the beginning by men who had travelled at their own charges, and toiled without monetary reward. It was a labour of love, a freewill offering of service for Christ's sake, and their brethren's sake. There had been many anxieties and troubles and fears by the way, but they had steered straight on, bating not a jot of hope or courage. And because they had fainted not, the fruit of their sowing appeared in due season, and the harvest ripened for the reaping.

Many of those who had first ploughed the field and scattered the seed did not live to see the glory of the harvest. As the years went by, those who followed in their steps were cheered by the signs of a rich increase; but even those who lived to rejoice in the good estate of the Association at the commencement of the last quarter-century could have had little idea of the prosperity and the developments which were to come. Truly, the best was yet to be, but the man who believed in it most, and who had given himself most to make it possible, was to share in the loved labour no more.

In the Aggregate Meeting at Newcastle-on-Tyne, in June 1925, William J. Back presented the Annual Report for the year 1924. It was the last Report he was to write, and the last Aggregate Meeting he was to attend. He had for a long time been carrying on his work under a severe physical handicap, and had suffered much pain. His gallant soul and his love of the brethren would not allow him to forsake his post, and he fought on to the last. He attended the General Committee meeting at Leicester in February, when he ought to have been resting on the South Coast with his wife and convalescent son. Soon after, he had a serious stroke, which deprived him of the use of his right hand.

It was the signal that his work was finished, and in the General Committee held at Hanley in June all hearts were saddened by the news of his resignation. In the Aggregate Meeting which followed, a special resolution was moved by Howell Mabbott, an ex-President, accepting the enforced resignation with profound regret, and recording the Meeting's unstinted and unqualified appreciation of the Honorary Secretary's twenty-two years of faithful service, which had contributed in no small degree to the marvellous growth of the Association during his term of office. As recognition of his great service, this beloved officer was unanimously elected as a Trustee, and the Aggregate Meeting's resolution was inscribed and presented to him in the form of an illuminated address.

In December of the same year, at a meeting of the

General Committee at Westminster, an enlarged framed portrait of our honoured colleague was presented to the Association by his wife and his sons, Hugh and Harold. Mrs. Back and Mr. Hugh Back attended the meeting, and the latter expressed the hope that the portrait would be accepted as a lasting memorial of his father's devotion to the Mutual Aid Association. The President, J. Simpson Alcock, accepted and unveiled the portrait, and referred appreciatively to its subject's unparalleled efforts and enthusiasm for the Association. Mrs. Back added a graceful word of thanks for the cabinet gramophone which had been presented to her by the Officers and General Committee.

Less than a year later, on 6th November 1927, William James Back passed away, and on the 11th, Armistice Day, his body was laid to rest in the new cemetery at Acton. A brief service was first held in the home, and then a large and representative company gathered in Acton Hill Wesleyan Church. The President, Samuel Smethurst, conducted the service and gave the address, Henry Bisseker offered prayer, and the lessons were read by Arthur Cowling and J. P. Williams.

So passed from the companionship he loved so much on earth one of the greatest of its number. All verbal appreciation of his dedicated life and work must be inadequate. As was written at the time of his death: 'He seemed to embody in his own person all that the Association stood for. Its life was his life; its progress and prosperity were his chief joy; and in its service he devoted himself with a single-hearted, self-sacrificing zeal which has rarely, if ever, been paralleled in its long history. The fact that out of the £450,000 which this benevolent agency has distributed in compassionate allowances, more than £200,000 have been raised in the last fifteen years, is a tribute to the greatness of the work accomplished under the inspiration and leadership of Brother Back.'

In the service of the Association he was speedily marked out for promotion to office. He attended his first Aggregate Meeting in Manchester in 1898; in 1902 he was Plan Secretary foı the London Aggregate Meeting, and in the same year was appointed an Honorary Auditor; in 1904 he was elected as one of the Honorary Secretaries; and in 1913 was designated as President-elect.

Apart from his unceasing general service, W. J. Back will be remembered for his responsibility for two innovations which have proved of use in after years. One was the institution of a breakfast for conveners in connexion with Aggregate Meetings. This function, at which he was so often the generous and genial host, was a happy occasion for conference and counsel for these important officials, and successive Honorary Secretaries have maintained the good custom when war-time restrictions have not prevented it. Another idea emanating from his busy brain was the contribution of notes by the Honorary Secretary in each issue of the *Local Preachers' Magazine*. Under the heading of 'Obiter Dicta' paragraphs of general and personal interest came from his pen every month. This admirable practice has also been followed by his successors.

But while his work for the Association merits fuller appreciation than can be given here, a brief reference must needs be made to the man himself, whom his friends and comrades knew and loved. A lion he was in fight for the interests of the Association, but he had the gentlest and tenderest heart of love for his friends, and for all in any kind of need. His spirit was gracious, his generosity was without measure. He was a noble Christian gentleman, and was as winsome an advocate for

John Harding

General Secretary 1883-1914

his Lord by his life, as he was by his earnestness as a preacher. William James Back has bequeathed a great tradition of service to those that come after him, and a name that will live as long as the Mutual Aid Association lasts.

It was fortunate for the Association that an Elisha was ready to take up the fallen mantle of the departed Elijah, and it soon became evident that the spirit of the lost leader rested mightily upon his successor. The first Annual Report from his pen, that for the year 1925, revealed Arthur Cowling as an adept in the writer's craft, and his proficiency in this kind was further evinced when, as Honorary Secretary, he took over, in April 1926, the task of supplying the monthly feature of 'Obiter Dicta' for the Magazine. But his literary ability was only a lesser part of his manifold gifts. It was the dynamic personality of the man that made him so forceful and vital an influence. He was a great captain, apt for leadership, and his manifest self-devotion to the task to which he had been called was an inspiration to all his comrades. Bright was the promise of the days to come with Arthur Cowling to lead and guide. Little did we dream how soon the beloved leader would be taken from our head.

In the Annual Report for 1929, the last that Arthur Cowling wrote, appreciative reference was made to the gift of a first mortgage of £40,000 on Belmont College, Wimbledon, better known as 'Southlands'. This munificent addition to our funds was the spontaneous contribution of Mr. Joseph Rank, and was offered by him as a mark of his gratitude and admiration for the services of Methodism's voluntary evangelists, the local preachers. This was by no means the first, nor was it to be the last, generous donation Mr. Rank had bestowed on the Association. He was ever a true and liberal friend of local preachers, and his name will always be remembered with grateful honour.

With such good friends, and such selfless leaders, the Association went on its way, blessing many and by many blessed. 'The affairs of the Association continue to prosper.' So wrote Arthur Cowling in his last Report. The note of triumph was justified, but he was to toil in the harvest-field no longer. A fortnight after the Aggregate Meeting at Manchester, he went to Shipley for the Branch anniversary. Returning to London on the Monday, he called at Head Office for a chat with his colleagues, the General Secretary and the present writer. The next day he was stricken down by an affection of the heart, and on 23rd June 1930 he died at the age of 62. It was a tragic, a stunning blow, a bereavement which was felt as a deep, keen sorrow throughout the whole brotherhood. He was a man of many facets, so vivid, so virile, so versatile, and always so kind and lovable, that his memory will long remain fresh and fragrant in the hearts of his friends and comrades. We knew that a prince and a great man had fallen in our Israel, and everyone mourned as for a brother beloved.

He was a man, take him for all in all,
I shall not look upon his like again.

A representative company came from far and near to Silsden for the funeral service during which the President, J. P. Williams, paid a touching tribute to the saintly spirit and whole-souled devotion of our departed colleague. Later in the year, as a further proof of his affection and esteem, the President presented a portrait enlargement of the late Honorary Secretary for the Association's possession, and he unveiled it at a meeting of the General Committee in December.

This tragic loss confronted the executive with the task of selecting and electing a new Honorary Secretary. In

1926, the present writer had been called from the editorship of the *Local Preachers' Magazine* to share the secretaryship with Arthur Cowling. As the junior partner in that office, the yoke had been easy and the burden light. To be saddled so suddenly with the load of full responsibility might have appalled a much better and abler man. It was fortunate that we had at the centre of affairs an officer so experienced and capable as W. E. Noddings, the General Secretary. Two are not always better far than one, but future events were casting their shadows before, and it was eminently desirable that a co-Honorary Secretary should be found. The hour brought forth the man. In June of the previous year, R. Parkinson Tomlinson had finished a brilliant term of office as President. He had come to the Chair with an added distinction as Member of Parliament, but the electors of Lancaster had forsaken their first love, and his career as a legislator had been cut untimely short. Westminster's loss was the Association's gain. On 18th September the General Committee with hearty unanimity appointed him to the vacant post, and his acceptance brought the Association an acquisition and an asset of untold value. 'Parkie', as Parkinson Tomlinson was affectionately called by his friends and brethren, was a man of singular charm and wide popularity, and he had proved himself an eloquent advocate and ambassador of our cause. In Conference and throughout the Connexion his standing was high, and the regard and repute in which he was held gave him an influence of infinite worth to the Association. His usefulness was soon to be put to the proof.

By this time, Methodist Union was well above the horizon; and it would not be long before it became an accomplished fact. In the same General Committee meeting when Parkinson Tomlinson was elected

Honorary Secretary, a sub-committee was appointed to investigate the position with regard to the admission of Primitive Methodist local preachers into membership of the Mutual Aid Association. This small, but important, committee consisted of the President, the Honorary Secretaries, Sir George Royle, Harry Dawson, William Edwards, R. Lindley, J. Morton Goodrich, J. H. Freeborough, and Thomas Currey. The question of Union was one which had frequently cropped up in the Association's meetings, and had commanded the general approval of the brethren. How could it be otherwise? Born in a time of discord and division, the Association had cared for none of these things, but in unity of spirit and the bond of peace brethren of varying sections of Methodism had laboured together in works of love and charity. They had found 'the tie that binds' in their common service of their common Lord, and anything that made for harmony and concord in the Methodist Israel must needs command their prayerful interest and earnest goodwill. Local preachers of sundry branches of the Methodist family were already participating in the fellowship and ministry of the Association. Could those who had experienced the blessedness of dwelling and serving together do other than hail with gladness the coming into one household of faith of all who sprang from the parent stock?

On 20th September 1932 Methodist Union was consummated in the Royal Albert Hall, London, the historic ceremony being honoured by the presence of Their Royal Highnesses the Duke and Duchess of York, now our beloved King and Queen. Thus the unhappy divisions, which for so long had kept asunder Christians who traced their religious ancestry to the same fount and origin, were healed. So vast a change in the constitution of Methodism obviously could not leave the Mutual

Aid Association unaffected. When the passing of the Methodist Church Union Act in 1929 practically assured the amalgamation of the three Churches, the officers of the Association devoted themselves to consideration of the most effective means of taking advantage of the impending change. The local preachers of the United Methodist Church already formed part of the constituent elements of the membership of the Association, and it only remained to discover a just and wise way of incorporating the brethren of the Primitive Methodist Church. The first step was taken by the Aggregate Meeting at Manchester in June 1930, which conferred on the General Committee plenary powers to negotiate terms of settlement with the Primitive Methodist Church. The Committee quickly got to work, and after prolonged and intensive deliberations transmitted its proposals to the governing body of that Church, on 13th November 1930. Throughout these preliminary discussions the desire, ever uppermost in the minds of the members of the General Committee, was to make the way of ingress for our Primitive Methodist brethren as easy and practicable as was consistent with due regard to the history of the Association, and the interests of its existing members.

It was plainly impossible to demand the payment of a sum which would be actuarially adequate for the admission of a potential new membership of over thirteen thousand local preachers. It became necessary, therefore, to discover a compassable 'goodwill' figure, which would enable the Primitive Methodist people to feel that they were making a worthy contribution, and at the same time would assure our own members that ample recognition was being accorded to the high standing of the Association, and the substantial benefits which the new members would be eligible to receive.

In determining this figure the Committee had regard to the sums paid when the Methodist New Connexion local preachers were admitted in 1896, and the Bible Christian local preachers in 1907, and the relation of such sums to the vested funds in those years. With these data in mind, and with the desire to go to the limits of generosity, the Committee proposed to the Primitive Methodist Church that a capital sum of £20,000 should be paid, in order to make all the local preachers of that Church eligible for membership in the Mutual Aid Association. In view of the increased annual expenditure which would have to be faced, it was made plain that the Association could only make this offer on condition that regular access to the circuits and churches for collections should be regarded as an honourable obligation, and that facilities should be provided for appeals for honorary members and subscribers. The proposal was cordially received and unanimously accepted by the Primitive Methodist Conference, with full appreciation of the generosity of the terms. A 'Lightning Effort' was organized to raise the money by an appeal to every circuit in that Connexion, and on 19th September, the eve of the Methodist Union, at a specially called and largely attended meeting of the General Committee, a cheque for the complete amount was formally handed to the Honorary Treasurer of the Association by the Rev. Jacob Walton, the General Secretary of the Primitive Methodist Church. Mr. J. Longstaff, the secretary of the 'Lightning Fund,' also attended, and in recognition of the great service he had rendered was elected a Life Member of the Association.

Following the Committee Meeting, the members were entertained to dinner at the National Liberal Club by the Honorary Secretary, R. Parkinson Tomlinson. The local preacher representatives to the Uniting Conference on the morrow were also invited. Sir George Lunn, Mr. Isaac Foot, then Minister for Mines, Sir R. Wilberforce Allen, and the Rev. Jacob Walton, the only representative of 'the cloth', were among the guests and after-dinner speakers. This happy function had the true eucharistic joy. It was a feast of thanksgiving, of communion and fellowship, of rejoicing in 'the dear uniting love' which had made brethren, too long divided, of one heart and one way.

When the 'goodwill' payment referred to above was proposed, the General Committee also offered to continue the allowances then being paid by the Primitive Methodist Local Preachers Aid Fund to more than two hundred brethren over the age of 75, on condition that the assets of that Fund were transferred to the Association. Such annuitants would be taken into membership without entrance fee or subscription. This matter was not proceeded with at once, but in November the General Committee received a request from the Primitive Methodist representatives that the original proposals relating to these permanent annuitants might be brought into operation. The Committee realized that the capital account of the Aid Fund had diminished since the date when the proposal was first made, but it decided to stand by its original offer, and agreed to accept responsibility for the regular annuitants of the Aid Fund on condition that the remaining assets were paid over immediately. The actual sum received from this source was £2,700. As the grants to these aged brethren totalled over £1,500 a year, a considerable addition to the Association's annual expenditure was thereby incurred. But because the Association, as our Primitive Methodist friends freely acknowledged, had been generous in its terms and brotherly in its welcome, it was confidently expected that they would loyally shoulder their share of the labour involved in raising and contributing the necessary income. It was the general belief that this enlargement of our borders would result in much blessing to all concerned, both in the extension of the ministry of comfort and cheer to needy and afflicted brethren and widows, and in the strengthening of the bonds of fellowship and brotherly love among the local preachers of the Methodist Church.

Immediate consequences of Union were the dropping of the designation 'Wesleyan' from the title of the Association, and the reorganization of the work in accordance with the District divisions as arranged by the united Church. In the Liverpool Aggregate Meeting of 1933 the President publicly welcomed the ex-Primitive Methodist brethren into the ranks of the Association. In responding on behalf of his colleagues, Charles Wass, of Birkenhead, thankfully acknowledged that, right from the beginning, the negotiations had been marked by fine Christian chivalry and brotherliness, and expressed his faith in the invincible potentiality of our great work. Certain requisite alterations of the Rules were made, including an increase in the number of General Committee members from sixty-five to seventy. It was further decided that the first additional five members should be chosen from the ex-Primitive Methodist section, and the following quintet were elected: Thomas Proud, John Walker, Charles Wass, Joseph Longstaff, and William E. Clegg. A year or two later, as a tribute to his outstanding services in facilitating and furthering the arrangements for fusion, Charles Wass was appointed one of the Association's Trustees.

Through the door thus opened to the Primitive Methodist brethren, a stream of new members swiftly began to flow. In the last three months of 1932 the number was 2,024, and 2,352 joined in 1933, making a total of 4,376 in fifteen months. In the first year after Union, collections in former Primitive Methodist churches amounted to £660, and in the following year this had grown to £1,441. The Report for the year 1933 showed that thirty-eight local preachers and five widows from that section were in receipt of weekly allowances, and in addition single grants had been made totalling £712, while the permanent annuitants had received £1,440. By 1934, the number of ex-Primitive Methodist local preachers and widows benefited by the Association's assistance had risen to 218 at a cost of £3,330, and £1,199 was paid to the permanent annuitants, a sum of £4,500 in all. When it is remembered that the average annual benefits paid out from the Primitive Methodist Aid Fund had been £2,159, it will be clear that the newly joined brethren had found 'an entrance ministered unto them abundantly' into this great and goodly fellowship.

CHAPTER NINE

AND THEIR WORK CONTINUETH

IT HAD LONG been the custom to send a message of loyal duty and greeting to King George and Queen Mary from the annual assembly of the Association, but in 1935 it so happened that the Aggregate Meeting was held in Westminster, on the anniversary of the King's birthday. It was also the year of His Majesty's Silver Jubilee. The usual telegram was felt to be inadequate to the occasion, and a loyal address of homage and congratulation was prepared instead. A collection was also taken in the meeting for King George's Jubilee Trust Fund, inaugurated by the Prince of Wales. The address and the contribution were duly acknowledged by the King and Prince Edward, His Majesty expressing deep appreciation of 'the sentiments of loyalty and affection'.

But little more than half a year was to pass, and then this gracious Sovereign and good and noble man was taken from his people. It was a bereavement felt as a personal loss throughout the Kingdom and the Commonwealth. The community of the Mutual Aid Association mourned him not only as King but as a true helper and friend of the poor and needy. The general sense of loss, which found expression in many ways, was summed up in the words which prefaced the Annual Report:

With deep and heartfelt sorrow, we record and mourn the death of His Majesty King George the Fifth. For fifteen years he had been a Patron of the Local Preachers Mutual Aid Association, and his gracious recognition and approval of our benevolent work gave great delight and encouragement to all our members. This practical sympathy with our service of charity was only one of innumerable instances of King George's love and care for those of his people who were in distress and need. He ever bore such in his kindest remembrance and goodwill, and sought to do them good. For his wide human sympathies, for the pure and noble example of his life, and for the Christian graces which informed his mind and heart, he is meetly and rightly styled 'King George the Good'. With the millions of his subjects throughout the Empire, the members of the Mutual Aid Association sorrow for the loss of a great and gracious Sovereign. They give thanks for his life of constant and faithful service of the Kingdom of God, and they will ever remember with grateful hearts His Majesty's kindly interest and help in the Association's ministry of brotherly and Christlike love.

The Report went on to assure Queen Mary of the tenderest sympathy and united prayers of all the members, and to offer to King Edward the Eighth their loyal duty and service, and their thanks for His Majesty's kindness in continuing the Royal Patronage of the Association. When King George the Sixth came to the throne some months later, the hearts of all were gladdened and encouraged when it was learned that His Majesty had consented to accord the Association the same high honour.

From the earliest days it had been the proud boast of the Association that, except for the necessary office staff, the administration had been carried on by the honorary service of men who voluntarily undertook their duties in addition to their ordinary avocations. So treasured was this tradition that a proposal to appoint professional auditors was by some received with 'a scornful wonder' as if indeed our precious unity were to be 'by schisms rent asunder, by heresies distressed'. But the vastly increased volume of income and expenditure, and the growing intricacy of our accounts, made it manifest that it would be wise to emulate the example of other Methodist funds, and secure an annual certificate from trained accountants. It was felt that this guarantee was due to the Methodist public who furnished the financial sinews of our work. The step was not taken hastily, but after nearly a year's deliberation on the matter, the General Committee decided in January 1935 that a professional audit should be the rule in future. The appointment of Honorary Auditors was continued, and in the Aggregate Meeting and the General Committee the state of the accounts is their peculiar charge.

Though the membership was steadily growing, it was a constant regret that so many local preachers had not entered into our fellowship. The Association had undoubtedly enlisted the great majority of active brethren, but there were numbers still outside to whom the benefits, both spiritual and financial, of sharing our service had not appealed. In order to remove a possible stumbling-block, the Nottingham Aggregate Meeting in 1936 agreed to suspend for one year the Rule requiring an entrance fee. It was 'not without dust and heat' that this concession was carried, for some of the stalwarts of the Old Brigade were little inclined to make less strict and strait the way of ingress for those who were foolishly blind to their privileges, or too selfish to help their brethren by uniting in this service of love. Though this dispensation did not produce as numerous a recruitment as was desired, it did have considerable effect. In the next two years an accession of 3,177 new ordinary members was reported, bringing the number of ordinary members up to 14,047, and the total membership rose to 23,841.

Ever appreciative of the sacrificial and selfless service of Methodism's local preachers, and of the benevolent work of the Mutual Aid Association, Mr. Joseph Rank bestowed a further token of his practical sympathy, in the early part of 1937, in the form of a munificent donation of £25,000. This splendid gift, so freely and spontaneously offered, was most cheering and welcome, and coming so soon after Mr. Rank's previous generosity, evoked the sincerest gratitude to our good and warm-hearted friend. The firm place the Association had won in the affection and goodwill of the Methodist people was made manifest by such gifts, and by the never-failing support of the friends in the churches. Expenditure also was growing, annuities alone in 1939 amounting to £27,927. The total benefactions of the Association in the ninety years 1849-1939 had well passed the million pounds mark, the figures being:

	£
Sickness benefit	216,242
Superannuation	790,359
Funeral Allowances	69,902
	£1,076,503

In addition to this, nearly £6,000 had been paid to the ex-Primitive Methodist annuitants in the years 1933 to 1939. Nor should we forget the distribution every Christmastide of gifts from the Stephenson and Wild funds, augmented by the bountiful contributions of loving friends. The help and relief brought to saints in distress by this ministry of loving kindness cannot be calculated in terms of pounds, shillings and pence. The spiritual comfort of this bounty is immeasurably precious, bringing as it does the assurance that the Church they had served had not forgotten them in their time of need.

The outbreak of war in September 1939 caused the evacuation of a large number of Government and business offices from London to the country. For the greater safety of the General Secretary's staff, and to ensure the uninterrupted carrying on of the work, it was thought prudent to take a similar course with the Association's office. A house was rented at Weybridge, the

Westminster chambers were vacated, and in the new headquarters 'business as usual' was gallantly transacted. It was not easy going, for the General Secretary had perforce to take up his residence in the same house, and the staff had to work in cramped conditions. But W. E. Noddings possessed the uncommon faculty of knowing how to sit 'calm on tumult's wheel', and with the cheerful co-operation of his clerks, everything was kept going in good order. Six years afterwards, when the war had ended, the period of exile terminated with the return of the office to London. The former rooms in Central Buildings were now denied to us, but the officers of the Methodist Missionary Society kindly placed at our disposal some rooms in the Mission House. Here a temporary lodging was found until, in March 1947, the office was transferred to its present habitation in City Road. In this connection, it is fitting that grateful acknowledgement should be made of the kindness and courtesy of Dr. Leslie Church and his colleagues on the Epworth Press, who have granted the use of their beautiful Board Room for the holding of meetings of the Association's General Committee.

The year 1939, which brought war and the beginning of illimitable woe and desolation into the world, brought also heavy and sore losses to the Association. Some of the greatest and best of our leaders and counsellors were taken from us by death. We lost four ex-Presidents: John Wesley Walker, Sir Thomas Rowbotham, Osmond O. Noel, and William H. Thornton, the two former of whom were also Honorary Trustees; three other Trustees, William J. Davey, Samuel G. Waddy, and John H. Freeborough; the Honorary Editor, Alfred England; and a member of the General Committee, George Orchard. The wealth and worth of loving service and saintly influence such a company of good men gave to their day and generation can never be told. Their names will be lastingly honoured, and their memories lovingly hallowed, as long as the Association lives.

While the income of the Association remained fairly steady during the war years, the expenditure on superannuation allowances, which constitute the bulk of our benevolence, experienced a serious decline. In 1940, the decrease was £3,509, in 1941 £3,011, and in 1942 £1,287. Needless to say, this sorry state of affairs was in no degree the desire of the responsible officers, nor was it due to parsimony in the administration. Its primary and principal cause was the coming into operation of a new Old Age Pensions Act.

This Act affected most of our annuitants of 65 years of age, and over, and in order that the recipients should receive the full benefit possible under the Government scheme, it was unavoidable that the Association's allowances should be brought within the scale which the official regulations permitted. The consequence was that, in the great majority of cases, a reduction in our grants became necessary. A collateral effect of the extension of State aid was a drop in the number of applications for annuities. In the widespread welcome and approval given to the State's practical recognition of its duty to care and provide for its needy and aged citizens, the Mutual Aid men could not but join, and rejoice over it. When the social conscience was unawakened on these matters, they, inspired by Christian love, had banded themselves together to help those who had no other helper. How could those who had shown and led the way in charitable assistance for the needy do other than greet with a cheer the community's growing awareness of the claims of human brotherhood?

But the effect of the new supplementary pensions was

certain to hamper and restrict our benevolent intentions and desires. The upper limit of the charitable grants we were allowed to make was *7s. 6d.* a week, and this obviously was bound to reduce the average of our allowances, which fell to *6s. 10d.* for men and to *6s. 4d.* for widows. It was not likely that so severe a crippling of our power to serve the needy would be accepted without seeking a remedy, or attempting to discover alternative means of extending a helping hand to our brothers and sisters in distress. Again and again the Assistance Board was approached with a view of securing a relaxation of the rigid limit to our grants, and after protracted negotiations the official regulations were modified so far as to permit of an increase of three shillings a week in the allowances made to local preacher annuitants. This concession had the happy effect of ultimately raising the average figure for men to *9s. 6d.* a week. Another way of help was found at Eastertide 1945 in a special gift of £5 to all our beneficiaries, a boon which brightened with added comforts the lot of many who were feeling the pinch of rising costs of living.

But it was evident that the time had come for more to be done if the Association was to fulfil to the utmost of its powers its mission of mercy and comfort to persons and families in need. Some amplification of the original objects was clearly called for, and in order to achieve this end a detailed examination of the existing Rules was undertaken. In this work the officers were favoured with the invaluable counsel and co-operation of Stephen R. Dodds, who had been President in 1940, and whose experience in his profession and in public life specially qualified him to advise in this complex task. A list of suggested alterations to the Rules was prepared, and these were approved at a special meeting of the General Committee at Westminster in March 1943 for submission

William E. Skinner

President 1902; Hon. Secretary 1904-1921

to the Aggregate Meeting at Nottingham in June. That Meeting heartily endorsed the proposed amendments, and so another historic step was taken in the progress of the Association. There was nothing revolutionary about the changes; they were all evolutionary, developments of the objects and design for which the Association was instituted.

The principal amendments were:

(*a*) Benefit members sickness pay was doubled, and their annual subscriptions ceased to be payable at the age of 65.

(*b*) Funeral allowance was raised from £4 to £10.

(*c*) Entrance fees were not required from new members below the age of 60, and the fees for entry after that age were substantially reduced.

(*d*) Granting of assistance in the form of lump sums, where such would be of more service than weekly allowances.

(*e*) Dependent relatives of deceased members were made eligible for assistance, which had hitherto been confined to their widows.

(*f*) Power was given to defray the cost of medical and convalescent treatment of necessitous members, and also to provide for attendance on the infirm and aged.

Beyond all this, dreams of establishing Rest and Convalescent Homes for local preachers were beginning to take shape, but except for the appointment of a subcommittee to explore the ways and means, nothing definite in that direction was done at that time.

The result of this wide extension of powers and benefits was speedily apparent in the returns of expenditure. By 1944 the benevolent grants had increased by £2,899, excluding a donation to the Red Cross of £1,000. Of this increase £867 was for superannuation allowances, which now totalled £21,188. In 1945 the expenditure under the latter head was £28,994. This included the Eastertide gift, and if this is deducted, say £5,000, an increase of over £2,000 remains. In 1946 the figure for superannuation was £26,690, an advance on the previous year of more than £2,500. Figures like these are a demonstration beyond any doubting of the need that abounds to be assisted, and of the comfort and benediction which the Association's ministrations bring. And for the further care of our old folk, the Association made a grant of £5,000 to the Methodist Homes for the Aged Committee, who have provided accommodation for a few of our members.

But while the Association was marching on from strength to strength, more of its trusted chiefs and leaders were falling by the way. On 3rd June 1943, two days before the Aggregate Meeting in Nottingham, R. Parkinson Tomlinson died. He was loved by all, and mourned by all with a grief beyond expression. A man of great charm and cheerfulness, he was a good companion and a generous friend. He was a distinguished son of Methodism, and had been Vice-President of the Conference. To only one other beside himself was accorded the signal honour of a second term as President of the Mutual Aid Association, a term which he left unfinished when he was stricken down. The memory of his bright spirit and radiant witness will be a light in the hearts of all his brethren for many a day.

Both Arthur Cowling and Parkinson Tomlinson died at the age of 62, and at the height of their powers. To lose the brilliant services of such men was a sore deprivation to the Association, and to the writer of the present history, who had been the colleague of both in the Honorary Secretaryship, the loss was a grievous personal bereavement. Both men had a genius for friendship, and their affection and sympathy were a strong tower and a priceless treasure. For three years no second appointment of Honorary Secretary was made, and then in 1946 after completing a strenuous year as President of the Association, Herbert Ibberson, of Barnsley, was prevailed upon to accept this further responsibility.

It was a piece of great good fortune for our organization, for complicated and formidable problems were looming ahead, and the new Secretary's legal experience and administrative ability would be of the utmost value in our councils.

A further great and notable change in the Association's executive occurred on 31st December 1946, when William E. Noddings retired from the post of General Secretary. For more than thirty-two years he had occupied this central position, and had made for himself a reputation and a name of exceptional brightness and distinction. In the performance of the intricate duties of his office, he was faithful and trustworthy to the minutest detail; as a preacher of the Gospel and an advocate of the Association in the pulpit and on the platform, his utterances were with spiritual force and convincing power; and in all his relations with his brethren and colleagues at Head Office and in the Districts, he displayed unfailing courtesy, sympathy, shrewd understanding, and sagacious judgement. He was a veritable 'guide, philosopher, and friend' to all, and he quitted his post with the assurance of the grateful affection and the enduring esteem of every member of the Association. As a mark of his brethren's loving regard for himself and their high estimate of his services, he was unanimously elected as an Honorary Trustee in June 1946. His successor in the position of General Secretary was Squire Jones, of Harrow, who assumed office on 1st January 1947.

CHAPTER TEN

EPILOGUE

THE EXIGENCIES of production demand that this history of the rise and progress of the Association shall be brought to a close before the hundred years of its existence are fully completed. But a survey of the present position and prospects reveals undeniably that constitutionally, functionally, and spiritually the Association is in good heart and health. Its place in the sympathy and goodwill of the Methodist people is assured, and witnessed by many signs and deeds of love. Among these may be cited the amount received from free-will offerings in the churches which, in 1947, reached the remarkable total of £19,979, a figure surpassing any previous contribution from this source. In the same year, the sum of £36,518 was distributed for benevolent purposes, the largest amount in our long history. Amazing figures like these would have filled the hearts of the founders of the Association with wonder, love, and praise, and those who are permitted to share in the glorious success and service of the latter days do so in humble thankfulness to Almighty God who has so richly blessed the labours of His servants, and crowned their efforts with His blessing and favour.

But although the ministries of the Association have been continually enlarged and extended through the years, yet wider visions of service have been conceived. The hampering restrictions of State regulations, which have obstructed the free and full flow of the stream of our benevolence, have to some degree been overcome by the opening up of new channels of relief, but a much greater expansion of our charitable care is now envisaged.

Provision for old age in its poverty and loneliness is becoming more and more a matter of public concern, and religious bodies naturally and of necessity are taking a practical interest in this philanthropic object. The Methodist Church is no whit behind others in this good work, and Homes for the Aged are now in being, and afford accommodation to many old folk of both sexes.

We have already noted that the Association has made a substantial grant to this Methodist Committee, and a few local preachers have become occupants of one or other of these Homes. But we have no control of admission and administration in respect of these establishments, and it is the Association's hope and desire that means may be found for setting up and maintaining Mutual Aid Homes for the care of necessitous aged and sick local preachers and their wives and dependants. To ensure that the legal proprieties are duly observed, the advice of the Association's solicitor, Mr. T. E. Chester Barratt, was sought, and his expert knowledge and guidance have been of immense value. After consultation with Mr. J. A. Reid, K.C., who drafted the requisite amendments to the Rules to make possible the achievement of our object, the General Committee submitted those amendments to the Aggregate Meeting in York in June 1947, and the meeting unanimously approved them. The purport of these alterations is to give the Committee power to establish Rest and Convalescent Homes for the sick, aged, or infirm members of the Association and their wives, widows, or dependants, and for the carrying out of this object a Company has been set up. An 'Association' numbering twenty-five has been appointed, all of whom are members of the General Committee, and from them an 'Executive' of twelve was selected. The new body, called 'Mutual Aid Homes Limited', has William Edwards as Chairman and the Secretary is William E. Noddings.

It is not necessary to stress how great a boon and benediction such Homes will be to our aged and afflicted brothers and sisters. Nor do we doubt that in this expansion of its benefits the Association will receive the generous sympathy and support of a host of friends in Methodism, whose gifts and goodness to us in the past have made possible this enlargement of our service.

While this spirit of loving zeal and ever-active ministry on behalf of others prevails, and while the purpose holds to serve, single-mindedly and sacrificially, asking nothing for ourselves, and doing all in Christ's name and for Christ's sake, the Mutual Aid Association will never fail to rejoice in the blessing of God and the bounty of kindly helpers.

Our record now is ended. It is a record of unnumbered mercies received and countless blessings bestowed, of a hundred years of sacrifice and service crowned with the loving kindness and goodness of God, of comfort and succour and joy brought to thousands of hearts and homes shadowed by sorrow and sickness, by poverty and need. Long as the tale of the years of the Association has been, not half has even now been told. Only a part of the host of heroic men who helped to shape the history of these wonderful years have been named in these pages. Many others there are of equal merit and devotion who have their memorial in the strength and beauty of the House of Mercy they laboured to build. Nor can the statistics of income and expenditure, the figures of membership, or the details of organization and administration, comprise the whole of the story. The Mutual Aid Association is infinitely more than a charitable institution. That has been true from its conception and inception until now. The first article in the first number of the *Local Preachers' Magazine*, issued in January 1851, expressed the conviction 'that the work in which we are engaged is approved of God, and calculated to confer great and lasting benefit on our brethren'. And the writer continued: 'We do not merely refer to the provision which it makes for the sick, or the pecuniary relief which it will afford; but to the good it will do to all connected with it, in the improvement of their temper, and piety, and devotedness, many pleasing instances of which we have already witnessed.' The note struck in the beginning has sounded clearer and clearer throughout our century-long history. The spiritual blessings resulting from this confraternity of preachers have been as real and precious as the benevolent benefits conferred.

The joy of selfless service of others, mutual encouragement and inspiration in their calling as preachers of the Gospel, and the nurture of the graces of the Christian character, these things are the rewards of those who share in this brotherhood of compassion. It may all be summed up in the great word, and greater experience, Fellowship.

Dr. Henry Bett, in his noble book, *The Spirit of Methodism*, says: 'There has probably never been, in the whole history of the Church of Christ, any community where religious fellowship was quite so real, or so deep, as it has been in Methodism. The bond of union was a common faith and a common experience.' The men of the Mutual Aid would add to that: 'and a common service.' Called first of all to be preachers of the saving truth and grace of Christ, and bound together in a common ministry of love and compassion to the needy for their Lord's sake, they have known a twofold bond of union which has been a constant joy and strength. So precious was this fellowship, that those who shared it in the earliest days declared that for this alone they would prize their membership in the Association. Thus it has continued to be through the following years, a fellowship of hearts and minds, bringing the brethren closer together in mutually helpful spiritual communion. Its value as a means of grace and uplift and inspiration to the whole body of local preachers cannot be overestimated. Methodism would be sadly poorer were her local preachers to decline, either in numbers or in spiritual power and zeal, and the Mutual Aid Association provides the only fellowship which joins them all together in a sacred unity of spirit and service. Under the auspices of the Association, week-end retreats for social and spiritual intercourse and conference are held in various parts of the country, such as Abbot Hall, Willersley Castle, Sidholme, Haywards Heath, to name only a few, and practical encouragement is given by the General Committee for the extension of these gatherings.

One in faith, one in fellowship, one in service, the Mutual Aid Association has reason to be thankful and humbly proud of its century of well-doing. It has been a helper of the poor and needy, and it has been, through its ministering servants, a mighty power in the Church in proclaiming the glorious Gospel of the Lord Jesus Christ. The reverend editor of the *Wesleyan Vindicator*, who, in 1851, beheld the fathers of the Association leagued with those who would either 'revolutionize or annihilate Methodism' need have had no fear. The only hope, desire, and aim of these good men was to show their love of God by loving their neighbour and tending their brothers in need. This is the foundation of the Christianity which is to bring the Kingdom of God on earth. On that foundation the Mutual Aid Association was built by good men a hundred years ago, and on that foundation it stands.

For their work continueth,
And their work continueth,
Broad and deep continueth,
Greater than their knowing.

PART TWO

The *Local Preachers' Magazine* and Character Sketches of Mutual Aid Leaders

CHAPTER ONE

LOCAL PREACHERS' MAGAZINE IN THE MAKING

THE AGGREGATE MEETING in 1850 decided that the Association should establish a magazine devoted to its interests. The first issue was published, as *The Local Preachers' Magazine and Mutual Aid Reporter*, on 1st January 1851.

Consisting of forty pages, it opened with a long, detailed, optimistic article on 'The Rise and Progress of the Mutual Aid Association'. Then followed a section headed, 'Essays, Scripture Illustrations, Etc.', in which a series of articles was launched under the general title of 'The Scripture Warrant for A Lay Ministry'. William Rogerson of the Royal Observatory, Greenwich, himself a local preacher and a member of the Association, began the 'Astronomical Notes' which for many years remained a notable feature of the Magazine. Our forbears were more intimately interested in the wonders of the heavens than we seem to be, perhaps because they had fewer earthly distractions. Rogerson, confident of that interest, began his contribution thus: 'Dear Brethren. While travelling to your country appointments in the evening of the first Sabbath of the new year, you will see the crescent moon approaching the western horizon, and thereby be led to contemplate the goodness of God, who hath appointed the moon to attend on our earth in its revolution round the sun, and by her mild and silvery beams to cheer the gloom of night, and by her powerful attraction to regulate the tides of the mighty ocean.' For many years such astronomical articles continued, with a judicious blending of factual statement and homiletical application, to combine scientific instruction with aids in sermon illustration.

In this first number also the precedent was set for the wealth of biographical detail which has characterized the Magazine all through the years. The life story of John Bristow, 'a local preacher in the Rochester Circuit for upwards of a quarter of a century', who had been born at Gorleston in 1789, set a good standard for such writing.

The remainder of the Magazine was devoted to reviews of books, letters to the Editor, an informative section on Temperance, a 'Miscellaneous' department consisting of brief quotations and articles, and—what was for long to remain a valuable feature—the 'Daily Remembrancer' so well loved by Victorians, with a text for every day in the month.

It was a good beginning. Well printed and set out, the Magazine was both useful for those who sought aid in pulpit preparation and entertaining for the general reader. Nothing was promised. There was no prospectus. The Editor was content to remain in the background. He did not even contribute an editorial article. Evidently he felt that the number should be judged on its merits, and he had good cause to believe those merits to be high.

That success rewarded his confidence is shown by the Report presented to the Aggregate Meeting held in the Surrey Street Music Hall, Sheffield, nine months later:

How far it has answered the expectation of the members it is not for your committee to say; but that it has tended greatly to advance the interests of the Association, they are bold to affirm—and the many instances in which donations have been sent, and honorary members added, clearly traceable to the perusal of its contents, encourage them to hope that it will not be allowed to fail for want of support, but receive increased circulation—that it may be made not only the medium of conveying intelligence respecting our progress to a greater number of persons, but ultimately a source of revenue.

A footnote to the Report opens a window upon another view. The Committee, it seems, 'have not thought it desirable to publish the accounts', which 'were submitted to the meeting, and were properly audited by persons appointed for that purpose'. However:

It having been insinuated, by parties who are jealous of our success, that those who promised money last year have not kept their word, and that £150 have been taken from the sick funds to keep up the Magazine, though we are not careful to answer such adversaries, we are desirous to reassure our friends, and therefore offer the following explanation. The promise of £200 was not made by individuals, but by a vote of the Aggregate Meeting, and it was intended to be raised by donations from individuals and collections in the branches. Of that sum, £74 19*s*. 6*d*. was sent in previous to the Report being read, and a sovereign has been received since then from Birmingham. We think this is creditable in the infant state of the Association. It was not expected that the whole sum would be paid the first year, and therefore a resolution was passed, empowering the Editor to borrow a sum not exceeding £200 of the Treasurer, to be repaid with five per cent. interest. Only £150 has been drawn; nor was that sum advanced all at once, but in three several fifties, and not until cash had been advanced out of the Editor's own pocket for months. Had there been any disposition to obtain funds from the Association, fully one half the amount advanced might have been charged for advertisements, etc., as is done by the *Methodist Magazine* and *Watchman* on the Missionary and other funds; but not one penny has been paid either for printing, paper, duty, or aught else; so that already the Magazine has given a large sum to the Association, and is in a fair way of paying back the whole loan with interest thereon. Let our friends help us to do this speedily.

That glimpse behind the scenes, answering questions that in differing forms have been asked at intervals ever since, shows how the enterprise was financed. The Committee added that, in its view, 'it is a matter for congratulation, that, with so many obstacles in the way, so respectable a circulation has been obtained during a year in which ordinary publications have been disregarded for those more immediately connected with the stirring events by which we are surrounded'. Those 'stirring events' included the ferment on the Continent following the fall of Metternich, 'the astonishing old gentleman', in 1848, culminating in France with the *coup d'état* by Louis Napoleon on 2nd December 1851, and leading also to the Crimean War. It certainly was creditable that at such a time a magazine devoted to the interests of local preachers should in so short a period firmly establish itself.

Nevertheless, as the Editor wrote in his introduction to the first volume, 'that Methodism should have existed for more than a century, dependent to a considerable extent on the labours of Local Preachers, without having an organ which they could call their own, appears strange in this book-making age':

> Yet so it is: for, with the exception of two or three attempts by private individuals, which proved failures, nothing was done either to acknowledge the services, improve the minds, or record the labours of these preachers of the Gospel of our Lord Jesus Christ.

The Magazine was printed by Petter, Duff and Co., of Crane Court, Fleet Street, London, and published by Aylott and Jones, 8 Paternoster Row. It had on its title page an emblem illustrating the text printed below it: 'Wise as serpents: harmless as doves.' The precise significance of the choice of such a text can now be only a topic for conjecture. Certain it is, however, that the first Editor quickly showed he had no special aptitude for applying it in his handling of the Magazine.

He was William Harris—later to become the Rev.

WILLIAM JAMES BACK

President 1914; Hon. Secretary 1904-1926

William Harris, D.D.—the first Honorary Secretary and also the first President of the Association. Born at Barnstaple, in North Devon, in 1813, he came of an old Hanoverian family, his father having crossed to England and in due time become naturalized. In 1843 the family moved to London. William Harris began to preach and happened to meet in the same class as the Editor of the *Wesleyan Times*, and it was largely as a result of that friendship, and much consultation between the two men, that the project of a Magazine for local preachers was put forward. Harris remained Editor until 1854, when he accepted a pastoral charge with the Wesleyan Reformers in South London.

It was a period of cataclysmic controversy within Methodism, and Harris was passionately on the side of the laymen who raised a standard of revolt at the 'reform' conference held at Birmingham in 1852. During the first year of his editorship he boldly plunged into the lists. He alludes to this, and the protests it evoked, in his Preface to the first volume:

The painfully afflicted state of Methodism has deeply affected us, and we have had occasionally to allude to it. To those who read with the determination to find fault, and who instead of reading or judging of the whole, take a passage from its connection and pass a verdict on it, our language may have seemed at times severe. We can only declare that our desire has ever been to be just. . . . None will rejoice more than ourselves when the breaches in our Zion shall be healed; and we pray to God to hasten the day when ministers and people shall have 'left off contention', and shall realize 'how good and how pleasant it is for brethren to dwell together in unity.'

It cannot be said, however, on the evidence of the pages before us, that he made any notable attempt to achieve that unity. He held strong opinions and expressed them with vehemence. This aroused bitter contention within the ranks of the Association and among the members of the Committee. Thus, writing from his home at 5 Waterloo Terrace, Islington, in December 1852, he says:

We have thought proper during the year to discuss some important questions in connection with subjects now debated between contending parties in the Wesleyan body. Our course in this respect has not been pleasing to some of our highly esteemed friends, and our defence is that, regarding our peculiar position as intrinsically neutral, and as, so far, fitting us to take a candid and dispassionate survey of the questions in debate, there was no impropriety in making known our view in the spirit of moderation and peace, and that in so doing the holy cause of truth, of justice, and of charity, would in some humble degree be promoted, and the reunion of separated if not estranged brethren be brought about.

Certainly he had a queer view of 'the spirit of moderation and peace'. In 1853, by which time the Magazine had been increased to forty-eight pages, he wrote a vigorous 'leader' dealing with what he described as 'a Connexional crisis such as has not existed since 1797,' and expounding the views of the Reformers. Crossing swords with the *Watchman* in subsequent articles, he argued that week by week it was throwing up barriers to reconciliation between parties. He supported the Birmingham Declaration which, among other things, asserted that the Wesleyan ministers' 'claim to an exclusive government of the Church by virtue of rights inherent in their office, is destitute of a scriptural basis, and repugnant to the spirit and letter of our constitution, the records of the Conference during the early years of the present century, and the known usages of our elder and larger societies in every part of the Kingdom'. He upheld the rights of the Leaders' Meeting, a mixed court of appeal, and lay election instead of ministerial nomination to Connexional committees, and supported the Birmingham attack upon 'the pastoral idea', the consolidating of 'power in the hands of the travelling preachers'.

There is no doubt that this forthright handling of

controversy had much to do with the swift success of the Magazine. Harris was a born journalist. If his courage and zeal outpaced his discretion, it was good for the journal's circulation. The Magazine was read and re-read, discussed, attacked, condemned. What more could its militant Editor desire? At the Aggregate Meeting of 1852, George Mallinson, of Huddersfield, declared: 'If it come to this, that I must either go without the *Local Preachers' Magazine* or go to bed without my supper, I would choose the latter alternative.'

Harris's wide intellectual interests, and appreciation of the catholic nature of his readers' outlook, are reflected in the varied contents of the early numbers of the Magazine. There was generous space for reviews of books, competently and critically handled. The 'Astronomical Notices' of William Rogerson were merged into a section on 'Science and Literature', and the same writer was soon contributing also 'Notices of Animated and Vegetable Nature'. Verse had a place, and lively correspondence. Other articles were grouped under such characteristic titles as 'Religious and Philanthropic Intelligence' and 'The Mutual Aid Association Reporter'. A further widening of appeal is indicated by the announcement that from 1853 the Magazine would be known as 'The Local Preachers' Magazine and Christian Family Record', a title that continued for many years. Explaining his reasons for this addition, the Editor declared:

> We desire to do good, especially to the household of faith: in order to do this, we seek admission to the bosom of the Christian families of our land, that Christian truth, Christian morals, and Christian experience—that is, principles and practice founded upon the plainest Scripture—may be disseminated, illustrated, and strengthened among English hearths and homes.

This fearless and independent journalist, however, who tilted with verve and animation not only at windmills but at Connexional leaders, was bound, sooner or later, to come into direct conflict with the official minds both of Methodism as a whole and of the Mutual Aid Movement. It must be said that the so-called 'mediation' articles from his pen read nowadays as if he had dipped his nib in vitriol. Journalism, both secular and religious, has changed greatly—and not perhaps always for the better—in the last hundred years. William Harris was a 'Thunderer'. No respecter of persons, he felt deeply and wrote forcibly. It is not surprising that before long he came under damaging fire in the Aggregate Meeting. He had been appointed Editor at a salary of £150 a year, and was subject to annual re-election. His policy was challenged in 1852. Some of his colleagues were gravely disturbed by what they regarded as his unwarrantable use of the Association's official organ for the thundering forth of his personal prejudices. As one critic put it during the heated debate:

> Allow me to say, it is within your province, whoever may be your editor, to circumscribe him within certain limits. He ought not to claim unlicensed freedom, and put in what he likes—certainly not. It is the organ of the Association, and, if any class of articles is thought to be opposed to the interests of the institution, he must bow to its decision. It does not choke his utterance on those matters, but merely says: 'You have no right to use the Organ of the Association to express your own private opinions.'

That is a point of view which has been brought out in every dispute with an editor of independent mind and spirit. Harris was not a man to be easily defeated by it. He defended himself with vigour, was reappointed, and went steadily on, walking perhaps for a while a little more circumspectly but presently launching further attacks. In the preface to the 1853 volume he declared:

> The completion of the Third Volume of the Local Preachers' Magazine is an event which its enemies predicted would never take place; but they have been proved false prophets.

By 1854 the circulation had risen to 6,000. The Editor, as would be expected, wholeheartedly supported the British cause against Russia when the Crimean War broke out. His leading article in June was headed: 'The Crescent and the Cross.' In it he wrote:

> England has a mission to fulfil in reference to these semi-barbaric States, which she can accomplish and Russia cannot. Hers is the march of enlightenment, of civilization—the spread of Bibles and missionaries—the diffusion of liberty and knowledge—the triumph of law and justice—the regeneration of peoples and institutions—the establishment of peace by the enforcement of the principles of the Prince of Peace. In His hands are the issues of this great quarrel.

The disputes concerning the Editor's liberty of action in the pages of the journal came to a head at the Aggregate Meeting in London in 1855, when for the first time it met in 'leafy June' instead of 'old October, bright and chill'. There was a great and often bluntly-spoken debate, at the end of which it was resolved: 'That a committee, consisting of Messrs. Carter, English, Cuthbertson, Chamberlain, Jameson, Chipchase, and Arter, be appointed to secure an Editor for the Magazine, at a salary of not more than £100 a year.' However, Harris's supporters subsequently succeeded in persuading the meeting to agree to the further resolution: 'That the appointment of the Committee is not intended to imply that the present editor is not eligible for re-election.'

It was, nevertheless, obvious that Harris's reign was drawing to its close. While for a time the controversy over the Reformers had increased the circulation, by 1857 it had fallen to 1,350. The price was then reduced to 2*d.*, which was felt to be the lowest the Association could afford, and the number of pages was reduced from forty to thirty-two. As a result of these measures the sales rose at once to 4,000.

The Editor conducted his magazine from a room at

the printers, now Messrs. Petter and Galpin, of Playhouse Yard, London, adjoining *The Times* office. He found his task to be increasingly difficult. He had lost the confidence of the majority of his brethren, and eventually he laid down his office.

His successor was George Boole Chaloner, of 2 Union Street, Union Square, Islington, from which the editorial work was to be carried on, with gradually increasing success, for many years. The printers also were changed. According to the imprint, H. Luxdale, of 38 Markham Square, King's Road, took over this responsibility 'at the office of the *West Middlesex Advertiser*.' Another sign of change was the announcement that in future the publishers would be Messrs. Partridge and Company, of Paternoster Row:

> Mr. Philip Parker, an active and prudent member of the General Committee, has undertaken to form and superintend the sale of the Magazine for the year 1858, and on behalf of the Committee will narrowly and minutely watch its interests.

He guaranteed that, except for the Editor's salary, not more than £50 should be lost on the Magazine during the year, thus silencing for a while the critics of the financial management. It was decided that every possible effort should be made to raise the circulation to seven thousand.

Harris had been too much absorbed in ecclesiastical controversy to notice the seasons of the Church year! Under Chaloner's direction, Christmas was for the first time in the history of the Magazine considered to be a suitable topic for a special article—but even then it did not appear until the January number!

The new Editor's course was not 'set fair', as he discovered at the Birmingham Aggregate Meeting of 1858. A member of the General Committee moved 'that the *Local Preachers' Magazine* be discontinued'. He did so, he said, because the society was in a failing state, and the Magazine was a tax upon its resources. In spite of the changes in the management, the deficiency was still about £50. He believed the Magazine had been improved, and ought to pay its way, but although extensively read, they could not gain for it enough popularity to make it pay. In the debate, others urged that if the proposal were adopted Honorary Members would be lost and the Association would suffer. The old issue of party topics was revived. Friends of the Magazine, however, rallied to its defence with such persuasive power that in the end there was only one vote in favour of the proposal.

For some years, nevertheless, the fate of the Magazine remained in the balance. In 1860 a delegate from Windsor declared that 'it would be a great burden off my mind, and a great relief to the Committee, to have done with the Magazine'. Yet later he moved that it be continued!

Chaloner—who, by the way, seems not himself to have been a local preacher—went quietly and steadfastly on. A man of poise and judgement, he was not easily discouraged by criticism. In 1863 at Manchester he fell in with the idea that the portraits of the Presidents of the Association should be printed, a practice that has been followed ever since. Gradually the enterprise justified itself. No longer were voices raised in Aggregate Meeting to urge its discontinuance. In 1864, after fourteen years of unselfish and untiring service, George Chaloner decided that in view of other business prospects the time had come to lay down the burden. In an article headed 'The Editor's Farewell' he declared, perhaps a little too complacently, that he felt himself 'free in every respect from the condemnation of accepting reward where it has not been earned'. He announced that he had made arrangements 'to join the indefatigable printer of the Magazine in his business', and thus would remain in association with the journal. A 'publication committee', he wrote, had been appointed 'to secure the editing of the Magazine gratuitously'.

In contrast to William Harris, he had kept studiously free from partisan controversy. As Editor he had been more peaceable, though not so distinguished or, in some ways, effective. Yet he had done what his more fiery predecessor probably could not have done—kept his paper afloat on strong seas and brought her into the quiet waters and the safe harbour. Thus ended the opening period of what was destined to be a long and not undistinguished career. The Magazine was firmly established. He handed it over to his successors as a going concern, full of possibilities, many of which were fulfilled in the long years that lay ahead. An editorial in 1865 admirably laid down the principles upon which all later editors have sought to build. The object, it declared,

> is not merely to supply knowledge and amusement to local preachers, nor yet to represent and advocate their interests only as a class. Its articles have embraced a wide range of topics, and its pages have abounded with useful information upon many subjects, adapted to general edification. The intention of its managers is, that it shall not only maintain its character as a domestic monitor, but that it shall aim at higher excellence, and be an efficient labourer in the field of literature, and a conservator of morals and of piety. The main object will be to do good to every class of readers. . . .

It was now published by Philip Parker at 8 Exeter Hall, Strand, and printed by Kent and Co., Simpkin and Co., and Stevenson, Paternoster Row. From then on the practice of employing the Editor at a salary ceased. The work was done for the good of the cause, in harmony with the service rendered freely all down the years by men and women who counted it an honour to be allowed to help their aged and impoverished fellow preachers not only without payment, but often at their own considerable cost.

George Boole Chaloner continued to take an active interest in the work until his death in 1880, watching over the interests of the Magazine as its printer.

CHAPTER TWO

THE MAGAZINE AND ITS EDITORS

THE EDITING of the Magazine had now been entrusted to an Editorial Committee, and on the whole this arrangement, which from many points of view was certainly not ideal, worked well. It seems clear that, as would be expected, in practice the responsibility was shouldered by one man, who was fertile in ideas, tireless in toil, and inexhaustibly patient. W. B. Carter had been a member of the committee set up to curb William Harris's activities some ten years before, and during the next decade he became increasingly the editorial executive.

Not all the efforts made to improve the readability of the Magazine found favour with the Aggregate Meeting. For example, experiments in fiction were attempted. Imaginary adventures of local preachers, which seem insipid today, were serialized. This brought heavy guns of criticism into bombardment. At York in 1867 one of the critics asserted that 'the insertion of imaginary tales was scarcely right in a religious publication. The fault of the age was sensationalism; exciting tales were one form of this, and we should guard ourselves against furthering it.' Glancing at these serials now, it can scarcely be thought that they were sensational. They certainly would never have brought a blush to the most maidenly cheek. However, W. B. Carter sprang to the defence with an enthusiasm worthy of a better cause. 'Much of Holy Writ', he said, 'is alike in character to our tales'— a claim which demonstrates to what a degree he had allowed zeal to outrun his judgement. 'So', he added, 'is the sublime allegory of John Bunyan. The teachings of our Lord were mainly clothed in fable, or parable.'

One of the debaters, who evidently had a sense of humour, declared—doubtless amid laughter—that 'the *Illustrated Police News* is a statement of facts, but the publication of such facts is a worse moral evil than any fiction ever written'. It was an amusing debate—or so it now seems; and the editors successfully defended their policy. The serials went on, but not for long. Doubtless the source of the stream dried up.

About this time the name of George Sims, which was to shine honourably in the annals of the movement, began to appear as a signature to devotional articles. His contributions became frequent. In 1873 he was appointed General Secretary of the Association.

Gradually the Magazine moulded itself to the changing needs of the age; for example, shortly after the establishment of compulsory education a series of articles was printed on 'English Grammar: Its Principles and Rules'. Preachers were realizing the need for more adequate equipment in facing congregations, the younger members of which would be better educated.

Finance was still a subject of controversy, but the problem was skilfully handled. During a discussion in 1871, the Aggregate Meeting was again reminded of the publicity value of the Magazine in making known the Association's benevolent work. 'The Association,' it was stated, 'like any other customer, is charged for the Magazine it uses and the advertising space it occupies', and the balance sheet showed a profit in 1870 of £15 18*s.* 3*d.*

In 1880 the office was moved from 19 Exeter Hall,

which had been purchased by the Y.M.C.A., to 24 Bedford Street, Covent Garden. Other changes were also pending. Some dissatisfaction with the editing was expressed at the Aggregate Meeting of the following year, and an amendment was carried to the proposal that the committee be reappointed. It was resolved that to the editorial staff should be added Dr. Aldom, J. Milsom, A. R. Johnson, and J. Lockwood. A decision recorded in the Report of the General Committee only two months later shows how difficult a situation that precipitated:

That Bro. Lockwood declining to act on the Editorial Committee, and it being found impracticable to carry on the Magazine with so large a staff, this meeting resolves that the three acting editors, and the three other old members of the Magazine Committee, be affectionately requested to continue their services; and that the additional names appointed by the annual meeting be kept as a list of reserve.

Little imagination is needed to appreciate what searching of hearts had occurred behind the scenes.

Since 1864 the work of editing had been divided among three men—W. B. Carter, T. Chamberlain, and P. Parker—out of a 'Publication Committee' of seven. It was clearly laid down that the three editors should read all manuscripts and determine what should appear, and that they should also make all the arrangements with the printer. But they were also under obligation to send all proofs to the other four, in the reading and correction of which they would thus have an opportunity to judge the articles and, if they deemed them objectionable, to express their views. This must have been a cumbersome and, it would seem to us, unnecessary complication.

However, in spite of all difficulties, the Magazine held to its course. A measure of its success is the fact that attempts were made from outside the movement to capture it for other interests. At the October meeting of the General Committee in London in 1883 it was reported that 'a minister, who was about to publish a new magazine of 48 pages, at 4*d.*, had written, wishing to absorb our Magazine into his; and then supply us on, what he considered, profitable terms with his new publication'. The cautious birds did not flutter into that not too craftily spread net. It was resolved 'that the General Committee has no power to enter into such negotiations without the consent of the Annual Meeting'. Doubtless they knew that the Aggregate, eager as it might be to criticize constructively, would not sanction such a plan.

Thomas Chamberlain, who had been appointed Chief Editor in 1864, and also occupied for twenty-eight years with resource and distinction the post of Honorary Secretary, resigned in 1885 and sailed with his family of eight children for New Zealand in search of health. A man of unusually strong personality and abounding energy, he had played a leading part in the notable progress of the Association. His quality may be judged from the fact that he had served as the Mayor of the Royal Borough of Windsor. He was President of the Association in 1856, and his untiring devotion to the cause is shown by the record that he had been present in the General Committee on 271 occasions. 'Discreet and straight, honest and prudent', he had guided the affairs both of the Association and its Magazine with great ability. In gratitude for all he had done, a testimonial fund was raised and he was presented with £500. In his place on the Editorial Committee there was elected one who was destined to take an increasingly influential share in the conduct of the Magazine—G. C. Amphlett, of Oxford.

Events rapidly left him virtually in charge. For in

1887 W. B. Carter died, and two years later Philip Parker resigned after serving for a quarter of a century. G. C. Amphlett then had only one colleague, J. Wesley Walker—another name to achieve lustre within the Association. This did not prove to be an easy partnership. When, at the 1890 Aggregate, the Magazine came under criticism, Amphlett said some readers wanted more articles and others wanted more reports—a situation repeated again and again in the history of the Magazine. He voiced his conviction that one man should be responsible for conducting it. Yet another delegate who was to become widely known, O. O. Noel, seconded this proposition, which was referred to the General Committee for further consideration. No action was taken. Criticism continued—there were many suggestions: some people wanted illustrations, others a children's corner, and others again would have preferred that all the space should be devoted to accounts of Branch and District activities.

In 1892 the General Committee set up a special subcommittee, and this recommended that from January 1893 the price of the Magazine be reduced to 1*d.* and that five thousand copies should be printed monthly. The question of advertisements was also reviewed, and it was decided to accept for one year an offer of £45 for five pages of advertisements—three on the cover and two facing the first and last pages of editorial matter.

At the Aggregate Meeting in Burslem, Staffordshire, in 1894, there suddenly appeared a figure from the distant past—the first Editor, now the Rev. Dr. William Harris. He came to every successive Aggregate for the rest of his life, and revived his early interest. But shadows were beginning to engulf him. He continued to preach until the end, and occupied a pulpit twice on the last Sunday of his life. The next day he collapsed at a meeting of the World's Temperance Congress, and died, aged 87, on 13th June 1900.

An attack on the Magazine was launched at Burslem by two delegates, A. Johnson and William Smith, who proposed: 'That the Magazine be continued as heretofore up to 31st December 1894, but that after that only the "Mutual Aid Reporter" be printed and circulated.' The critics brought powerful artillery to bear, and it seemed for a while that they would demolish Amphlett's defensive positions. However, he and his colleagues averted defeat by agreeing that the problem should be referred to the General Committee. This proposal was made by W. E. Skinner—then a rising debater on the floor of the house. His suggestion was that efforts should be made to see if amalgamation with some other magazine might be arranged.

This idea greatly interested the Rev. I. E. Page, for a breakdown in health had led him two years previously to give up the editorship of *The King's Highway*, for which he had been responsible since 1872. In the interval he had served in a country circuit, and his health had been fully restored. His heart was in journalism, for the exercise of which he had undoubted gifts, and he saw an opportunity to return to its adventures. He lost no time in calling upon W. H. Stephenson, of Newcastle-upon-Tyne, the President-elect, to lay before him a proposal to save the Magazine. At first, with Skinner's project in mind, Stephenson thought Page wanted to join the *Local Preachers' Magazine* with *The King's Highway*. 'Not so,' said Page. 'But I want to help in any way I can.' He realized the value of the Association's work, and believed that it would be a grave mistake to jeopardize the future of the Magazine.

A meeting with Amphlett was arranged and the two men agreed to co-operate. Page began his long series of contributions under the pen-name of 'Jonathan Dale'. The relationship, however, was not solidly founded. Amphlett, it would seem, was not easy to work with; perhaps, indeed, it was too much to expect that in all the circumstances the plan should succeed. At the Newcastle Aggregate the next year, under Stephenson's chairmanship, another long discussion took place on Magazine affairs. Amphlett explained with engaging frankness that while his personal relations with Page had been cordial he could not continue, as he felt that only one man should be Editor. Page, who had led a deputation of Wesleyan ministers in an earlier session, listened to the debate from the gallery, and eventually saw Amphlett's editorial colleague, J. Wesley Walker, elected co-editor with himself (Page).

This was a revolutionary decision, but proved to be a wise and profitable one, for Page had a natural flair for journalism. The gift seems to have run in his family, for his brother, Jesse Page, a Nottingham local preacher, edited with distinction two magazines, *The British Workman* and *The Band of Hope Review*, and wrote biographies of Spurgeon, John Bright, and Bishop Pattison. I. E. Page, it transpired, had actually made his first journalistic appearance in the *Local Preachers' Magazine*, having contributed, as he said, 'some crude thoughts in verse' to its pages. His active editorship continued for fourteen years. On his retirement it was written of him: 'Orthodox without obscurantism, and modern without disloyalty to the faith once delivered, he proved himself guide, philosopher, and friend to many a seeker after truth.' His service to the Magazine was varied and unstinting. In addition to shaping policy, he wrote for it sermon outlines, articles, and notes; gave sound advice, was always ready to help the Association, or any young preacher who wished to learn how to write. He

Arthur Cowling

President 1922; Hon. Secretary 1924-1930

never obtruded himself, but was a brother among brethren. At times it has been suggested by ill-informed critics that the Mutual Aid movement had at least a strain of anti-ministerial prejudice. The story of the Rev. I. E. Page's cordial and long-continued fellowship with its Cabinet is surely an adequate reply.

He once gave his readers a revealing glimpse of his editorial method. 'In the writer's study', he wrote in the December number, 1907,

> is a drawer, into which goes everything pertaining to editorial work. Nothing sent is overlooked. When the time comes for the Magazine to be made up—25th of the month but one before its issue—the contents are opened out, and the number arranged. Sometimes an article is kept a long time till it fits in, because special care must be taken that each number, in varied contents, may be an harmonious whole. Among most valued helpers must be mentioned Bros. W. P. Parkin, R. Lindley, and W. Lethaby, who revise the 'proofs' every month. Every 'proof', it may be said, passes twice through four hands.

W. P. Parkin, of Gateshead, co-operated also in other ways. For many years he collected 'News From Far and Near', being responsible for this useful section of the Magazine. William Lethaby was a scholar who could have secured for himself a good worldly position, but he felt a call to spread Christianity among the Arabs in Palestine. Moab was especially laid upon his heart, and after thrilling adventures he settled down in Kerak (the Kir of the Old Testament). From there he sent articles about his work to the Magazine. He had lived in Frome for many years before he heard this call, and undertook personal responsibility for a Methodist cause in a village seven miles away, walking there and back every Sunday.

On a visit to the Orient he was impressed with the need for Christian work in Moab, and with characteristic courage, he became a solitary witness-bearer, gathering the children together and teaching them about Jesus, and gaining the goodwill of even Mohammedan fanatics. Eventually he returned to his home in Wiltshire and resumed his work as a local preacher. He then devoted his high intellectual gifts to the service of the Magazine, and for many years corrected the proofs with conscientious care. He moved to Devon in later years, and died there.

Under the guidance of these devoted men the Magazine prospered abundantly. In the 'Jubilee Year', 1899, the contents were rearranged. The Editors announced 'new arrangement, new wrapper, new type, and, we hope, new inspiration'. Readers were encouraged to write. Book prizes were offered for the best articles on 'Dr. Parker's Autobiography' or 'The Life of Dr. Moulton', and for the best five hundred-word letter on set topics. Neat, well-drawn, Victorian page-tops and drop-letters embellished the pages. The Magazine had regained its prestige, and faced the turn of the century with a confidence that was fully justified.

Page and Walker worked together in the closest harmony. It had been laid down by the Aggregate Meeting that Page, 'a literary gentleman of great experience', should undertake 'under the guidance of the present Editors' the management of the Magazine, 'of course, gratuitously'. At first there was some friction, as could only have been expected. It was contended by J. Bamford Slack that the scheme drawn up by Page had not been carried out. Finally it was decided that J. Bamford Slack, G. J. Morris, and W. E. Skinner—all notable in the progress of the Association—should 'arrange with the Editors and Mr. Page for the future management of the contents of the Magazine, and that it be an instruction to the Sub-Committee that they should adopt the plans already approved by the General Committee during the past year'. Walker, in contrast to Amphlett, approved the scheme and desired to allow Page a free hand in carrying it out.

J. Wesley Walker, of Maidenhead, was a man of wide experience in business and a preacher of outstanding ability. A magistrate and chairman of the Maidenhead Board of Guardians, he was attracted to the Mutual Aid movement by reading Philip Parker's autobiographical tract, *Grandfather Johnson*. He was elected President in 1897, at the age of 48. His fertile pen was active in the pages of the Magazine, to which he contributed a lively regular feature headed 'Look Around'. A series of his articles was republished by the Aggregate Meeting's instruction as a pamphlet, *Stories of Help*. He continued as Editor until 1904, when he was succeeded by James Kerry.

Page undoubtedly made a lasting impression upon the Magazine, and his work was highly appreciated. He continued his active control until the first World War, and indeed never ceased to take an interest in it right up to his death in 1926. He was in many ways a 'character'. A keen fisherman, he loved to dally on the banks of a country stream. When he set out on a day's fishing his wallet would invariably contain bait, a meagre lunch, and a choice volume. And, real disciple of Izaak Walton though he was, he never felt he had spent the day well unless he had gathered some fresh bait for his work as a 'fisher of men'. Many a 'catch' from those solitary meditations appeared in the pages of the Magazine. He was, also, we are told, a delightful companion on a country ramble or in the home. He used to say that the one thing for which he looked in any article submitted to his judgement was—fire. He retired, at the close of his long and tireless day, to Sleights, and there enjoyed a beautiful sunset. He was always on the look-out for contributors who would impart freshness to the Magazine, and one of them he found in his own circuit—the illustrious Richard Lindley, one of the doughtiest champions that ever enlivened the General Committee. And he it was who joined Kerry in the editorship when Page laid down his responsibilities.

Kerry also was a man of remarkable calibre. Born in 1847, he was a Methodist by birth and ancestry. It is said that John Wesley preached in his grandfather's barn. He early showed a taste for literature and music. Studious by nature, and having notable gifts of speech, he was greatly influenced as a youngster by the winsome and cultured evangelism of the Rev. F. W. Macdonald, at Trinity Church, Redland, Bristol. He became a local preacher before moving to Plymouth, where he was active in the life of the Free Churches, rising to the Presidency of the Three Towns Free Church Council. There, and later in London, he served the Church as class leader and steward, maintaining his interest also in choir and Sunday school. He was a master of the craft of preaching, and fashioned a felicitous style both in speaking and in writing that reflected his questing mind and understanding heart and gave to his words a persuasive power of high quality. Never effusive, he had great reserves from which at the appropriate moment he could draw both wit and wisdom.

His editorship reflected those qualities. Personal glory was no part of his editorial ambition. The Magazine in his day benefited greatly from his careful, precise, analytical mind. His standing is indicated by the fact that when he was living in Bristol he was invited by the Quarterly Meeting to take the place of Morley Punshon, then at the height of his powers, while that celebrated preacher was away in Canada for several months. Kerry did so with conspicuous success, refusing to accept any remuneration. The circuit showed its appreciation by presenting him with a copy of the *Encyclopædia Britannica*.

The Magazine gives no sign of awareness of the tragedy that was to engulf the world in 1914. Indeed, the August number for the year, prepared in July, makes no reference to war. In September appeared this comment:

> When the brethren were so peacefully in session at Sheffield who could have dreamed that the great Armageddon was close upon us? War, horrid, awful war, who shall depict its agonies, its devastation, its hideous tragedies? . . . But the word of God standeth firm. What a duty we have to the people! Our God is the God for such a time as this. Ours is the God for emergencies. One good old saint said the other day, 'I have found my God to be a wonderful God!' That is it! We have a wonderful God, and the people need Him. The times cry out for the living God, and it is ours to proclaim a God superior to all emergencies.

A message from the President, W. J. Back, called the preachers to prayer and the preaching of 'the great truths of the existence, and salvation, and sovereignty of God'.

That note was sustained throughout the trying years of war. Conditions of publication became increasingly difficult. Paper supplies were curtailed. The Magazine had to be reduced to sixteen pages. It did not, however, suffer in quality. Much of the praise for that great service must be awarded to James Kerry, although he did not himself survive the conflict. He was taken ill in 1916, and his chair was occupied temporarily by the Honorary Secretary, W. E. Skinner. The hope that Kerry would recover was not fulfilled, and he died in the September of that year.

It was then that there came to the helm of the Magazine one who has had more influence than any other in fashioning the policy of the Association, and steering it through the by no means easy waters of the last thirty years. F. Harold Buss was appointed Co-Editor with

Richard Lindley. The step was taken at the General Committee in Birmingham on 21st January 1917. Welcoming him in the March number, Lindley wrote:

It is a particular pleasure to have Bro. Buss as Joint Editor. For some years he has been gradually growing in the favour and esteem of his brethren, and while his voice is seldom heard in our meetings, his pen has often served us, and those delightful character sketches under the title of 'Mutual Aid Miniatures', now appearing in our Magazine, have revealed a facile pen, and a shrewd analytical mind, which makes his brethren glad to secure the constant service which as Joint Editor he can and will give.

They were prophetic words. Before long F. H. Buss's trenchant comments transformed 'The Editor's Chair', and in the very first number which appeared under his joint editorship 'Obiter Dicta' made its bow. At first, however, the paragraphs were signed 'W. J. B.', and, beginning modestly, W. J. Back thus introduced the feature: 'The Editors have commandeered me for a few paragraphs each month on matters of interest relative to our Association.' It was not until 1930 that 'F. H. B.' took over—from 1926 it was written by Arthur Cowling; but it is evident that the idea was his, and since 1930 it has been the most eagerly awaited feature in the Magazine.

An interesting event which foreshadowed later developments occurred during this year. In the November Magazine there appeared correspondence on Church Reunion between Howell Mabbott of Penzance, a Cornishman of charming personality who graced the Chair of the Association in 1920, and A. E. Hills, of Richmond, Surrey, who put the Anglo-Catholic point of view. Mabbott had written to the *Methodist Recorder* on the subject. In reply Hills said:

Your anxiety about the possible disappearance of the lay ministry is fortunately unfounded. To us Anglo-Catholics it would be of the first importance to preserve the entire structure, customs, and organization of Wesleyan Methodism. That is the meaning of the taking into the Church of England of the Methodists 'as a body'. Though I am what I fear you would call a very high Churchman, yet I believe that such an organization as the Wesleyans have is precisely what is wanted in the Anglican Church. I cannot say that, in my opinion, laymen should govern the Church, but that they should have special duties and functions assigned to them would only add to the strength of the Church. My view of the absorption may be expressed in such an answer to a supposed question as: 'Yes, the sermon today was preached by a Wesleyan', just as in ancient days the answer might have been: 'Yes, we had a Dominican to preach last Sunday'. It would be the Wesleyan Society within the Church.

Howell Mabbott replied that in his opinion such an arrangement would not be possible, and he strongly upheld the view that Wesleyan Methodism was not a 'body' or a 'society', but a Church. The situation foreshadowed by that correspondence has in recent days again emerged as a topic of serious discussion.

Those who have known both Richard Lindley and Harold Buss realize that the partnership of two Editors so dissimilar in temperament cannot have been easy. It survived, however, until 1920, when, in the December issue, F. H. B. announced his colleague's resignation and paid graceful tribute to his work as Editor. At the Aggregate Meeting in Bradford in June of the following year F. H. Buss was appointed as the sole Editor, the Association thus returning to the excellent practice abandoned nearly seventy years earlier. A shadow of coming events appeared in the number in which that appointment was made—E. T. Waite, of Salisbury, who was to succeed him, wrote his first article for the Magazine.

An indication of returning prosperity was the increase to twenty-four pages, and the striking progress of the Association was fully illustrated in the vital and challenging contents.

A glimpse of the tribulations that beset the pathway of an editor is afforded by an apology to his readers printed in December 1924. 'A serious misfortune' had overtaken him, the bulk of the copy for that number having gone astray in the post. 'Productions from our pen, the fruit of many hours' study and labour, have disappeared', announces this modern Lamentation, 'along with paragraphs, obituary notices, and other matter.' A major disaster indeed! One can readily imagine how sorely tried were even the improvising resources of F. H. B.

In 1925 the Magazine was increased again in size to thirty-two pages, at which it has remained ever since. History was made during the following year: it is recorded that on 17th January the President, Dr. T. E. Nuttall, broadcast from Birmingham in a service arranged with the B.B.C. by the Conveners, W. Sturmey Wolverson and A. E. Deed, who read the Scripture portion.

The Honorary Secretary, W. J. Back, suffered a seizure in 1926 and was reluctantly compelled to resign. At the Hanley Aggregate, F. Harold Buss was unanimously elected to succeed him, and felt he must relinquish the editorship. His influence, like that of Harris and Page before him, left a permanent impression upon the Magazine; he gave to it an atmosphere of literary distinction as well as the precision to be expected of a Government official. When these high matters were decided in the Five Towns, Arthur Cowling said that as yet no name was available for the editorial succession, and the General Committee was empowered to ponder, weigh, and act. It appointed E. T. Waite, of Salisbury, a journalist by profession, whose policy, choice of material, and lay-out of the Magazine reflected the charm and consideration that have endeared him to all his brethren.

Like all other editors who are worth their salt, he occasionally had to face storm-clouds of criticism. Perhaps the hurricane was the controversy which followed an article on evangelical preaching by Ellis W. Heaton, a North-country schoolmaster who shared Arthur Cowling's modern theological convictions. The Editor had to defend from the platform of the Aggregate Meeting both his contributor and his own independence. 'The Magazine certainly gives official information about the Association's work and position and needs', he said,

> but it does not set up any one to speak *ex cathedra* on matters of faith and doctrine. We have no Pope. We think and let think, and we welcome any articles from Methodists that are calculated to be helpful to our readers. We are grateful to brethren who take the trouble to pass on the considered result of their reading and thinking and praying and working, whether we agree altogether with their opinions and methods or not, as long as the article appears likely to be useful and stimulating in the work we all have at heart.

The Association rightly upheld his independence, having full confidence in his judgement.

It was under his editorship that 'F. H. B.' took over responsibility for 'Obiter Dicta'—in August 1930. His incisive, courageous, yet always courteous and graceful writing lifted the feature to new heights of glory and made it the most widely discussed contribution.

After nine years E. T. Waite laid down his office on being appointed Editor of the *Salisbury Times*, an influential weekly newspaper on the staff of which he had served for many years. Alfred England, of Leamington, was invited by the Aggregate Meeting to fill the vacant chair, and he did so with dignity and devotion until his death in 1939. His cultured mind, careful judgement, wide business experience, and broad and liberal outlook enabled him to uphold the traditions established by his predecessors. He contributed many thoughtful articles himself, generous in tone, graceful and felicitous in style; and, avoiding controversy, gave to the Magazine a quiet, modest, reflective atmosphere that was widely appreciated. He had first addressed the readers of the Magazine in June 1901 with a characteristic sermon on John 15, 11, writing in his charming way upon 'the joy of the Man of Sorrows'.

On the brink of the second World War the General Committee appointed as his successor R. G. Burnett. After the fall of Dunkirk and the beginning of austerity in the affairs of the nation it was decided that, to avoid drastic curtailment in size, the Magazine should be published not every month but every other month, an arrangement which unfortunately had to be continued for a much longer period than was then envisaged. However, in spite of many and great difficulties, the periodical has appeared regularly and maintains a circulation higher than at any time in its history. It looks forward confidently to the celebration of its centenary in 1951, when perhaps it will offer to its readers, as in its first issue, some reflections upon 'The Rise and Progress of the Mutual Aid Association'. If that be so, the note of thanksgiving will be: 'What hath God wrought.' Having called into its service a company of men and women of diverse gifts but one over-riding loyalty, the Magazine may be said to have served with some distinction a great and glorious cause.

CHAPTER THREE

'THE FATHERS, NAMED IN STORY'

THROUGHOUT the hundred years of its career the Mutual Aid Association has won the unreserved allegiance of a host of preachers whom no man can number. They have been drawn from widely differing walks of life. Their gifts have greatly varied. Rich and poor, educated and uneducated, barristers and judges, carpenters and cattlemen, journalists and men of business, Members of Parliament, mayors, councillors, artisans, labourers—all have had graces of character and culture in the presentation of the Gospel. All found their inspiration in the love of Christ for the last, the least, and the lost; and sought to serve Him by applying to their aged and infirm brethren His precepts of charity and succour.

In this and the following chapters it is proposed to recall the life and character of a few of these leaders in the movement. The task of selection has been difficult. For every one mentioned here it would be possible to mention a thousand. The willing servants of the Association have been in number as the grains of sand upon the sea shore. We choose merely a few examples to illustrate the wealth and diversity of those who have spent themselves joyously in a cause that evoked their devotion.

One of the earliest was James Wild, of North End, London. Born in 1782, he was the twelfth and youngest son of an active and industrious tradesman who lived near the middle of Union Street, in the parish of St. Saviour, in that department of London known as The

Borough. His quality and determination were revealed when he fell in love with the daughter of a man who exercised business in both London and Hull. When her father carried her off to Hull, James Wild followed her—on foot! He set out to walk the whole 197 miles. On the first day he walked until he was exhausted, and then lay down and slept at the side of the road. The next morning fortune favoured him, for as he rose to resume the journey a town-and-country carrier came along, took a fancy to him, and gave him a lift for the rest of the way. Alas, the lad's enterprise was in vain! The girl's father packed him off back to London.

After a while, however, he fell in love with another girl, and married her. But, says the quaint Magazine record, 'to realize unbroken matrimonial felicity was not his lot'. 'Death disturbed his quiet, and took away the desire of his eyes', and the cruel blow was repeated a second, a third, and even a fourth time. They were all, it seems, 'loving and beloved, worthy women and excellent wives—so excellent that he could not reconcile himself to widowhood'. So he married a fifth, 'a lady not less tender and attached to him than the preceding ones had been', and she survived him. Who shall deny that here was indeed a remarkable man?

Brought up at Surrey Chapel, he was converted at an early age and wrote out, and signed, a solemn covenant with God. In 1799 he apprenticed himself to a citizen of London and when he had served his time wanted to start out in business for himself. He bought a small shop and was about to complete the agreement when his mother had a strange dream. 'Her sleep was disturbed one night by the appearance of her deceased husband, who held before her a gold ring, encircled with the words of Isaiah 27, 3: "I the Lord do keep it; I will water it every moment: lest any hurt it, I will keep it night and day." The ring of gold then crumbled to dust, leaving the words still legible. He then, looking earnestly at her, said: "Take the hint—act upon it", and disappeared. The next morning she desired her son James, at whatever sacrifice, to desist from his scheme, part with his lease of the premises, and return to his master. Sadly disappointed and mortified, he nevertheless yielded obedience to his mother's wishes, and Mr. Hunter gladly received him.'

Some years later he did set up in business as a woollen merchant on his own account, and prospered abundantly. His character in business as in Church affairs was marked by integrity, perseverance, practicality, and uprightness. He helped to establish the first Sunday school in connexion with the Hexagonal Chapel, built by John Wesley, in Crosby Row, Borough. There he worked without stint, joining a band of Methodists who went through the district, street by street, and brought into the school the children of the poor.

In 1807 he received a letter from Dr. Adam Clarke asking him to call upon him. He did so, and received this advice: 'I wish you to give yourself particularly to prayer and reading. Besides the Bible, which should be your daily study, read Mr. Wesley's *Appeals*, his *Life of David Brainerd*, his edition of Baxter's *Saints' Everlasting Rest*, and Mr. Fletcher's Works.' Dr. Clarke had perceived his quality. He encouraged the young man to preach. More than that, he went himself to hear him preach his first sermon at Woolwich. Indeed, so highly did the doctor think of him that he tried to persuade him to join the itinerant ministery, but Wild's mother discouraged this, thinking that his constitution was not sufficiently strong, and on hearing this Dr. Clarke advised him not to take the step. He became Dr. Clarke's executor.

Wild was one of the small group of men who founded the Mutual Aid Association, and he was elected President in 1854. An impressive and earnest preacher, he occupied the leading pulpits of the Connexion. He was a forceful evangelist and had great moral courage. He would face hostile crowds with equanimity; in those days it was no easy thing to be a Methodist preacher. When paying toll at a gate, he would exclaim: 'Think of your soul.' He established himself at North End in a beautiful mansion, within its own enclosed garden and spacious grounds. Nearby he built a chapel, calling it 'Ebenezer—stone of help'. When it was complete, he offered it for the use of the Connexion, but retained it as his own property. After the expulsion of the three ministers by the Conference of 1849, he was one of those who signed the Birmingham Declaration following the conference presided over by Sir John Ratcliff. He allowed some of the expelled preachers to use his chapel, whereupon the Wesleyan preachers were withdrawn. He then made the chapel over to the New Connexion.

James Wild served the Association from the beginning as its Treasurer. He objected strongly when nominated as President, pleading deafness, but the Aggregate Meeting overruled him and appointed the Ex-President as his deputy and assistant. He delivered from the Chair at Bristol in 1855 one of the most memorable addresses in the Association's history. His good works were uncountable, and included the establishment of a day school near his house, which he maintained at his own expense.

Another leading personality of the earliest days was Isaac English, the second President. Born at Stevenage, in Hertfordshire, in 1794, he was taken at the age of two to Enfield, where his father kept a country inn. While the child was still very young his father died, and the mother carried on the business. She saw to it, however, that her children were taught religion. On Sunday evenings the parlour was regarded as sacred, and while drinking went on in the tap-room she would teach her children the lessons and prayers of the Church of England service.

At fourteen Isaac was apprenticed to an Enfield baker. Until his conversion he had little mental culture. He lived the usual gay, drinking life of the time. At 24, however, he lost his job. He went back to Stevenage, came under good influences, and began to go to church. Later he settled at Greenwich, joined the Wesleyans, and, like James Wild, entered into a written covenant with God. He drew up a document of four clauses, surrendering himself and consecrating all he had, and solemnly signed it. Then he began to serve in the Sunday school, and visit the sick. In 1820 he became a 'public exhorter'. He diligently studied the Scriptures, discovered in himself a gift for preaching, and in 1823 was accepted for the Deptford Circuit Plan, which included Greenwich.

He had married a year before that, and founded his own business as a baker and confectioner. He opened his shop for the first time on a Saturday morning. His first customer, buying a half-quartern of flour, said: 'I suppose you mean to open your shop on Sunday?' Promptly he replied: 'We intend to take God at His word, and keep holy the Sabbath Day.' This astonished her, and she exclaimed: 'What, then, do you think you are doing here? Why, the people who were here before you could not live even by baking on the Sunday. I won't have anything to do with a baker who refuses to do that.' But he would not compromise. He maintained his principles; and, in spite of all the gloomy prophecies of his critics, soon built up, and maintained, a prosperous business. In twenty-three years he was able to retire, and for ten years he gave himself wholly to religious and philanthropic work.

Notably successful as a class leader, for many years, it is recorded, he had few short of a hundred people regularly attending his classes. They were 'well fed with spiritual food', wrote an observer. 'They were *led*, not driven.' He prayed in secret for them every morning. His zeal as an evangelist made him take his stand week-by-week in the market-place at Greenwich adjoining the infirmary of the magnificent Hospital; and weather-beaten pensioners, the veterans of many battles, crowded to hear him gladly. He always invited them to come to the chapel, and he and his friends would lead the way, singing. On Sunday afternoons he preached in the open-air at Blackheath. Often, also, he would respond to invitations to go on board the ships and preach to the sailors. His chief concern was to spread abroad the tidings of the Kingdom.

He did not spare himself in preparation. A keen student, well acquainted with the literature of Methodism, especially the hymns of Charles Wesley, he had a mind stored with intellectual treasure; but always his chief text-book was the Bible. He learned enough Hebrew and Greek to read the Scriptures in the original languages, as well as the critical works of lexicographers and philologists. Having a clear grasp of Methodist doctrine, and a gift for clear exposition, he could hold his congregations spellbound.

The Birmingham 'Mediation' Conference of 10th December 1851 had Isaac English among its members, and during the disputes which divided Methodism many members of his classes were cut off from the Church, as a contemporary commentator says, 'by the summary mode of withholding their tickets at the

R. Parkinson Tomlinson, J.P.

President 1928 and 1942; Hon. Secretary 1931-1943

quarterly visitation, for the discontinuance of their usual contributions for the support of the itinerant ministry. Their leader thought it right, notwithstanding this, to continue to meet them as usual, regarding such a mode of exercising the discipline of a Christian Church as essentially despotic and unscriptural, and therefore null and void in all its acts'. He therefore absented himself from official meetings, preached a special sermon for the 'Reformers', and was summoned to answer charges at a Leaders' Meeting. This he refused to do. The meeting was so ill-attended that it was felt advisable to adjourn it. When it met for the second time, however, 'all the male members, except two', were present, and on 17th May 1852 it was resolved 'that Bro. English cannot continue to hold the office of a class leader amongst us with advantage'. It was further recorded 'that Bro. English is no longer considered a class leader in this society, and that he be requested to give up his class books'. To this he responded with a reasoned argument, refusing to comply. Of the class book he said: 'I beg to say it is my own; I bought it and paid for it. I will cast up the money and forward it to the steward.' This he did, and thereupon joined the 'Reformers'.

These echoes of battles far away and long ago fall strangely upon modern ears, but they show that such men as Isaac English had marked and independent personalities. His evangelistic and pastoral work merits appreciative notice. One of his class members for over twenty years was Captain Morgan of the missionary ship *John Williams*. He continued until the end of his active and fruitful life his close association with the Mutual Aid Movement, which had the vision to refuse to perpetuate within its ranks the divisive quarrels. Indeed it was in the Editor's room that he was suddenly seized by the illness from which he died on 28th November 1855.

Equally celebrated among our founders was Philip Parker, born in 1803 in the cottage of an agricultural labourer at Shipley in Sussex. His father died when the boy was only three, leaving a widow and eleven children.

In those days of George the Third there were no good schools or cheap literature for the poor. But Parker was made of no common clay. After a hard childhood and adolescence, he left the country to seek fortune in London. There, by what he always regarded as the leading of Providence, he found lodging with a Methodist who held a class meeting in his house every Sunday afternoon. The lad joined it. In 1821 he received his first ticket as a member on trial at Southwark Chapel from the Rev. George Marley.

Those were the days of cottage prayer meetings, and soon he became a prayer leader, a teacher in the Sunday school, a distributor of tracts, and a local preacher. Before long he was leading a class of his own, and then also a second; over three hundred members passed under his pastoral charge.

He also was in at the beginning of the Mutual Aid Association. He was present when the meeting assembled in Hart's Temperance Hotel, Aldersgate Street, London, to discuss its formation, and was at once elected as a member of the committee, representing London, charged with the arrangements for the first Aggregate Meeting. Before long he was appointed to serve on the General Committee, and continued to do so until 1893.

A man of lively convictions, he was, during the subsequent Methodist strife, in his own words, 'whirled to the front of the Reform Movement'. Of strong character, he was inevitably a centre of the storm. 'I was deposed as local preacher in Southwark Vestry', he wrote, 'for taking part with the Reformers, December 1850, and expelled the Society for the same fault, March 1851.' He then joined the Wesleyan Reform Connexion and, with the Rev. J. Everett, compiled the *Reform Hymnbook*. In 1853 he became the Connexional Editor and Book Steward. When he assumed these responsibilities he had no capital, having to build upon a foundation of faith alone; yet when he handed over his responsibilities twenty-three years later he recorded a gross profit for the year of £3,000 and stock-in-hand valued at £500.

It is remarkable that the agitation which rent Methodism and involved such strong characters as English and Parker did not shake the fellowship of leaders of the Association. When in 1864 it was decided to appoint a committee to assume editorial responsibility for the Magazine, Philip Parker was one of those elected, and he rendered invaluable service both in editing and distributing. Over a period of twenty-five years he was a constant and voluminous contributor. His work included a metrical version of the Forty-second Psalm, serials and essays innumerable—in all at least 1,200 pages, a record exceeded only by W. B. Carter. For all this he received no payment whatever. When he had to cease such literary work the General Committee acknowledged its debt to him by presenting a testimonial and a purse of money. He then entered the book trade, opening in Bermondsey a business as 'bookseller, stationer, binder and printer: hats, caps, and Dutch clocks supplied'. The practice of Philip Parker and his wife was to read every day a passage from the Old Testament in the morning and a chapter from the New Testament in the evening. On the advice of Dr. Adam Clarke, they thus read the whole Bible, 'hard names and historic chronology, nothing was missed'. In 1893 his wife died, and the old man did not long survive that blow. His call came on 24th June 1895, nine days before his ninety-third birthday. Shortly before, he had given the bulk of his large collection of books to the Salvation Army.

W. B. Carter was born at Lenton, near Nottingham, in 1802, in a poor but godly home. His schooling was scanty; little more, indeed, than that which he picked up at a Dame's School, where, as a small boy of more than average intelligence, he soon learnt all the 'Dame' could teach him. At a very early age he was sent to work in the lace trade 'as it was considered desirable that he should be initiated into habits of industry early in life'. For a while he attended a Church of England Sunday school, but his father died and when his mother married again, his stepfather, a Free Thinker, gave him no encouragement to continue.

At the age of fifteen his uncle sent him out with an older man as a commercial traveller in North Wales. Within four years he had set up a promising business of his own. When twenty-one he went to a Methodist watch-night service at Halifax Place Chapel, Nottingham. The experience impressed him so much that, to quote his own words, 'when all the congregation were bowed in silent prayer to God, he struggled for salvation, and found peace'. Joining a class meeting, he soon was its leader. His travels took him to many different parts of the country, and he began to visit the chapels. The societies soon recognized his value, and asked him to pray. Then came a day when at a village on the road from Oswestry to Welshpool he was suddenly invited to preach in the open air. It started to rain heavily, and a waggon-shed was procured, and in it he preached with great acceptance to two hundred people. At this first attempt he preached for an hour from John 3, 16! What better proof could any man have of a call to preach?

That was in 1823. Soon afterwards he was accepted as a Wesleyan Methodist local preacher. His facility was remarkable. It is said that he never preached the same sermon twice! He became a tireless student. Early seeing the importance of accuracy in grammar, he set himself diligently to master it, and ceaselessly impressed the need for such study upon his fellows. He also took private lessons in Greek and Hebrew. And later, when as a man of means he was able to travel, he also mastered Italian.

When his branch of business was affected seriously by revolutionary changes in the lace trade, he retired, and devoted himself to religious and philanthropic work, including twenty-two years' service on the editorial committee of the Association's Magazine. In 1861 he visited Geneva for the Evangelical Alliance. He wrote and published books on religious and Sunday school themes, including a history of the Nottingham Sunday School Union when he was its Jubilee President in 1855.

He was a typical serious-minded product of the generation, sound in judgement, an untiring worker, optimistic though always restrained, and, fearing to seem frivolous, more severe in appearance than was ever necessary. His profound and critical knowledge of Scripture was always at the service of his brethren, either in the Magazine or in oral discussion. A man of deep devotion, lively intellect, and shrewd insight, the secret of his power lay in diligent, humble prayer and continual study. He died in 1887.

Dr. Joseph Rufus Aldom, M.A., Fellow of the College of Preceptors, another of our honoured founders, was the son of a Wesleyan minister, the Rev. Isaac Aldom. He was born at Holsworthy, Devon, in 1821, and educated at Kingswood School. For nine years he served as Senior Master of Taunton School, until in 1857 he moved to Leyton, East London, as Principal of Salway House College for Young Gentlemen and of the College for Young Ladies at Cambridge House, Capwith Street. His liberal outlook, tolerance, high-mindedness, and unsectarian vision marked him out as a leader among men. He served the Association devotedly and was elected President in 1876. He did much to weld the movement into a forceful unity.

The first General Secretary of the Association, Edward Creswell, was a Loughborough man, born of a good family in 1794. His mother, a staunch Baptist, trained him in the rudiments of Christianity. His parents, however, both died before he was fourteen, and for ten years he lived gaily and heedlessly. Misfortune then overtook him. He suffered a considerable loss of property, and had to change his way of life. Then it was that his early training turned his mind to more serious reflection. He was living in London, and joined the Wesleyan Church, eventually beginning to preach. With three others—W. Bowron, W. Harris, and W. Nash—he sent out the invitations to the exploratory meeting at Hart's Temperance Hotel, in Aldersgate Street, when he was chosen as the Honorary Secretary, a post he retained until the Association's Rules had been adopted and printed.

His enthusiasm and devotion to duty impressed his colleagues, and in 1850 he was appointed General Secretary at a salary of £80 a year, out of which he had to find his own office, 'devoting himself entirely to the Association's interest'! There is no doubt that the continued and increasing success of the movement owed much to his patient, business-like work. He was prompt in dealing with correspondence, persistent in pressing the Association's claims, and clear in exposition of its aims and achievements. For many years he lived in Abbot Terrace, Knightsbridge, and was a faithful worker in the Chelsea and Hammersmith Circuits. After the death of his wife, he moved to Mitcham, where he joined the Church of the Free Methodists in the village.

In 1869 a sudden stroke curtailed his physical activities, but even then he was indomitable in his determination to continue his responsibilities. Although bedridden and incapacitated, he taught himself to write with his left hand, and carried on. Being unable to attend the meetings, he relinquished a quarter of his salary; but to the end he continued to keep the account books and watch over the Association's business.

George Sims, who succeeded Creswell as General Secretary, was another remarkable personality. Born in 1811 and converted before he was seventeen, he soon began to preach and to teach in Sunday school. He came to London in 1840, joining the Islington, City Road, Circuit. Five years later he moved to St. Marylebone, and he served the Hinde Street Society for over forty years. Transparently honest, his ready sympathy for the poor and needy made him an ideal advocate of Mutual Aid philanthropy. He had uncommon versatility, was widely read, and his remarkable memory enabled him to make the fullest use of his reading in both preaching and writing. Over a long period he contributed many articles to the Magazine. The last appeared after his death in the number dated December 1882, and characteristically discussed 'The Distinction between Conversion and Entire Sanctification'. His clear grasp of doctrine and his lucidity of expression made him an advocate of the first rank.

A very different man, though in his own way as able, was Joseph Howarth, the blind town-crier of Oldham. Blind from his birth, and poor, he yet became a Wesleyan preacher. For forty-three years he 'cried' official news in the streets. He died, aged 75, in 1862, and was so highly respected that a statue was erected in his memory in the Alexander Park. A correspondent in the Magazine once described a pilgrimage he made to the park during an Aggregate Meeting. 'I was somewhat disappointed at first,' he wrote; 'for the statue shows the brother to be blind, wearing a tall, ugly, badly-worn old hat, a rough old coat with large buttons, and other garments equally worn and of an antiquated cut; in one hand he holds his bell, and in the other his faithful hooked stick. Indeed it is a representation of the man in his work-a-day attire, and not as he was when, dressed in his best, he offered the blessings of the Gospel in our chapels, from a mind richly stored with Bible truths, and being able to repeat from memory the lesson for the day, and all the hymns, as accurately as if he could read them. Coming from a Borough which clothes its town-crier in a coat embroidered with gold, and a hat to correspond, I thought that this Corporation was only perpetuating the memory of its own parsimony and meanness, in thus representing our old brother.' However that may be, it is evident that Joseph Howarth, in spite of grievous affliction, won the esteem and affection of his fellow citizens. In his latter days he received a pension as a Mutual Aid annuitant.

Thomas Bateman, of Chorley (1799-1897), was a friend and colleague of Hugh Bourne, William Clowes, and John Wedgwood. With them he carried on with zeal and fervour the evangelistic campaign in the first half of the nineteenth century which brought into being many village societies and chapels. The endurance of these early Methodist preachers passes our comprehension. Here is a typical example. Thomas Bateman, who was a farmer, left the reapers in the cornfield at half-past five one Saturday night, hastily changed, and walked six miles across country to Burwaldsley to conduct a service in a quarry late in the evening. A local farmer insisted that, instead of walking back home, he should stay the night in the farmhouse. Next morning he walked three miles to another hamlet, after refusing all food except dry toast and a glass of milk. He preached at Brown Knowl and held a prayer-meeting there; then he went on to a society just outside Nantwich to 'improve' the death of one of the leaders. From there he walked home to be ready for milking at half-past five on Monday morning. Nearly thirty miles on foot, with four services, two of them in the open air!

Self-taught, he was a great reader, and although not a scholar he was wonderfully versed in general knowledge. Short sight had excluded him from sport, and all his leisure—which was little enough on a farm during the period of the Peninsular War—was devoted to preparing his mind and heart for his service as a preacher. He was a good farmer and a pioneer in the co-operative movement. He became the Chairman of Directors of what is thought to be the oldest Agricultural Co-operative Society in England. Frequently during disputes concerning agricultural conditions he was called in as a mediator: 'Leave it to Bateman,' the disputants would say, 'he'll settle it between us equitably.' He was, in fact, a court of appeal on farming affairs for half a century.

Devoted Methodist though he was, he also served for many years as Churchwarden of Wrenbury Parish. His handling of finance was masterly, and his concern for the material wellbeing of the incumbent led him to raise a substantial sum of money and with it purchase a farm, the rent from which augmented the inadequate stipend. His public spirit also led him to become a pioneer among the Guardians of the Poor. The high respect in which he was held is indicated by the fact that before his death the new chapel in his native village was named 'The Bateman Memorial Chapel'. When he died, the Tunstall District Mutual Aid Committee erected a monument in the churchyard, and the inscription refers to him as 'an associate of Hugh Bourne, and one of the fathers of the Primitive Methodist Church. A man mighty in word and deed'.

He farmed on the estate of the Marquis of Cholmondeley, himself a man of great piety who, in the third quarter of the nineteenth century, conducted a religious service at the castle every Sunday evening when he was in residence. The Marquis was a deep student of Scripture and a fine preacher. His services always attracted large congregations. Frequently the Marquis invited Bateman to take his place when he was unable to preach himself. The two men also went together to Bible meetings, and at one of these a galaxy of 'stars' was completed by the presence of the Bishop of Chester. When the notables had delivered their souls, the Marquis quietly said: 'I feel sure the audience would like to hear a few words from a layman; will my neighbour, Thomas Bateman, address the meeting?' When the farmer sat down, after a masterly discourse, the Bishop chided the Marquis for 'having so adroitly manœuvred our total eclipse in this fashion by foisting upon us without warning his favourite tenant'. Bateman's exploits as a preacher were prodigious. Once he walked seventeen miles from Chorley to Chester for morning service, then three miles to a village afternoon gathering, back to the city for the evening, and home—in all, forty miles. Racy, humorous, courageous, having a natural grace and dignity, he could hold vast crowds, and was the first preacher allowed to speak in the open air at Wrenbury without being assailed with rotten eggs and fruit.

A great character also was Joah'n Preston, of Yeadon, in Yorkshire. It was his chief delight to take part in meetings for testimony, and it was no unusual thing for him to walk ten miles to conduct a Methodist Lovefeast.

On one memorable occasion he was announced to lead such a feast at the village of Harewood, between Leeds and Harrogate. The Earl of Harewood had heard much about Joah'n, and was anxious to hear him, but could not bring himself to go to the service in the little Methodist Chapel. When one of the servants, a devoted Wesleyan, told his master of Joah'n's visit on the coming Sunday, the Earl said: 'You must bring him to the house, and tell him that her ladyship would be pleased to hear one of their prayer meetings.'

So on the Sunday afternoon a party of five went to the castle. They were led through a labyrinth of passages, and eventually were brought to a stand opposite the sitting rooms. Joah'n, filled with inspiration from the lovefeast just held in the little chapel, gave out the hymn: 'Rock of Ages, cleft for me.' They sang lustily, so moved that tears ran down their faces, and then prayed one by one. Joah'n closed the meeting with a most beautiful prayer. 'It seemed', said one who was present, 'as if he'd chosen the daintiest bit out of every prayer he had previously uttered.'

When they got up from their knees the Earl and the Countess went up to Joah'n, each placing a hand on his shoulder, and said: 'We have no need to ask which is Mr. Preston. Your prayer is sufficient identity. We are pleased to have the opportunity of making your acquaintance.' They slipped into his hand two five-pound notes, and asked him to meet the Earl at nine o'clock the following morning.

But Joah'n, though deeply grateful for such kindness, replied: 'If it please your lordship, I cannot make any appointment for Monday mornings. Perhaps you may not know, but I've got a grown-up family, and they are all spinners and weyvers at home, and on Monday mornings I seek the work in for t'week.'

'Oh, I see,' said his lordship. 'But you must stay at Harewood tonight, and I will send you home in one of the carriages in time to do your business.'

So it was arranged. Joah'n slept at the home of the Master of Harewood Hounds, and met the Earl at the appointed time the next morning. The Earl showed him round his piggeries, and when they came to a fine litter of young pigs he invited his visitor to pick two of them for himself. 'If it please your worship,' said he, 'they are sadly too big for a working man; they would starve him to death trying to feed them.'

'Very well, then,' was the reply, 'we'll go to a lesser breed.'

Joah'n chose two fine animals, which were sent on to him the next day.

A few weeks later the Earl paid him a visit, and said he thought the pigs were ready for feeding. Soon after, he sent two bags of potatoes, one sack of sharps, and two sacks of oatmeal. Joah'n, far from having his head turned by such bounty, ascribed it, as he did all good things, to the goodness of his Heavenly Father.

It is fitting to conclude this chapter on ancient worthies with a note on a tragic event which drew a noble tribute to a local preacher from Lord Tennyson, Poet Laureate.

Sunday morning, 26th December 1886, Boxing Day, was among the wildest on record in the Isle of Wight. Ministers and local preachers had to battle their way to appointments against biting wind and driving rain. One veteran local preacher, Isaac Porter, after struggling to win his way through, fell dead within a short distance of the Wesleyan Chapel at Freshwater.

It chanced that within a few minutes Lord Tennyson, whose country home was near by, came upon the scene with his friend Professor Ralston. He was much impressed with the tragic event and showed his sympathy by interesting himself in the preacher's widow and friends. Among the circumstances that moved him was the fact that, as the dead preacher's notes revealed, his sermon that morning was to have been of an especially joyous character. Tennyson, reflecting on the honour and blessedness of the preacher's voluntary calling, wrote to the widow:

'I cannot but look upon his death as a happy one; sudden, painless, while he was on his way to his chapel to render thanks and praise to his Maker. Our Liturgy prays against sudden death; but I myself could pray for such a sudden death as Isaac Porter's.'

After recording this incident in the Magazine for April 1893, the Editor adds the following note, quoted from Henry J. Jennings' book, *From Lord Tennyson*, as indicating the poet's interest in Nonconformity:

While his form, it is said, has not darkened the doors of the parish church for many years, one of the Haslemere tradesmen, who is a

Nonconformist village preacher, tells with much satisfaction how he once numbered Lord Tennyson in his audience. He was going over Blackdown on a preaching visit, and, having started somewhat earlier, rested on a bank to rehearse his discourse, as he thought, to the summer breeze. On nearly reaching its conclusion, he found, to his surprise, that he was not alone, for on the other side of the bank there were Tennyson and the Duke of Argyll. They had evidently been listeners some time, but finding their presence was noticed made off as quickly as possible. It is to be hoped that the 'seed did not fall into stony ground', for it must have been the only sermon that the poet had heard for many years.

CHAPTER FOUR

'SOME OF THE GREAT ONES GONE'

Judge Samuel Danks Waddy (1830-1902) was the eldest son of Dr. Samuel D. Waddy, who became President of the Wesleyan Conference at Manchester in 1859. His influence within the Mutual Aid movement saved it from what might have been disaster. Born amid the tumults of the division that shook Methodism to its foundations, not a few of its early leaders, as we have seen, associated themselves prominently with the seceding groups. In these circumstances it is not surprising that the fathers of Wesleyan Methodism should have regarded the Association with suspicion.

That situation was changed radically when S. D. Waddy joined the movement. It was a Northampton local preacher, Bro. Durley, who made the first move. He travelled to London and went to see the distinguished barrister in his chambers in the Temple, and there presented the Mutual Aid case. Durley himself must have been an advocate of remarkable persuasive power. He convinced the shrewd laywer, answered all his probing questions satisfactorily, and enlisted his support. That was an epoch-making day in the Association's history.

S. D. Waddy was one of the leading barristers in the country and became Recorder of Sheffield, and a Liberal Member of Parliament, before being appointed as a County Court Judge. The fact that he was a Methodist local preacher did not help him in promotion, but he would not give up a vocation which to him was the most important of the services he had felt called to render his generation. A Bencher, and Treasurer of his Inn, he gave himself unsparingly to the cause of the Mutual Aid. For many years he was a Trustee and a member of the General Committee. In 1870 his brethren delighted to honour themselves by electing him as President. Throughout his maturity his speeches were a leading feature of the annual Aggregate Meeting. It was well said of him that he was the Association's 'ablest advocate'. In addition to all his other work, he wrote a notable *Harmony of the Four Gospels*. His last testimony was simply: I have kept my firm faith in God to the end.

His leadership and wise guidance brought the Mutual Aid into the sun of Methodist approval. He will ever remain one of its foremost, and highly revered, captains. A movement that could attract and hold the allegiance of such a man needs little other commendation.

Throughout its long story the Association has been served magnificently by many lawyers of great ability who have placed their experience, learning, and forensic abilities freely at its command. This perhaps is an appropriate place in which to write of two or three others who may be taken to represent a host of their brethren.

J. Bamford Slack, born at Ripley in Derbyshire in 1857, when he became a local preacher, followed in the footsteps of his father. In 1868 he entered the Wesley College, Sheffield. He graduated B.A. at London University in 1876, and in the following year was articled to Mr. Samuel Leech, the Derby solicitor, later serving with Leech's London agent, F. C. Greenfield, in Lancaster Place, Strand. Admitted as a solicitor in 1880, he practised for nine years in Derby, taking a prominent part in the life of that community and becoming a member of the first Derbyshire County Council. In 1890 he moved again to London, having acquired a partnership in Monro, Slack and Co., of Queen Victoria Street.

Meanwhile, in 1877, he had been accepted as a Wesleyan local preacher. As soon as he came south he joined the West London Mission, and almost at once Hugh Price Hughes secured him as his circuit steward. Before long, he was taking the Sunday afternoon conference at the St. James's Hall when Hugh Price Hughes could not be present. Tall, broad-shouldered, with his fine moustache, domed head, and piercing, twinkling eyes behind pince-nez, he was a commanding personality. His interests ranged widely from the law to cricket, from theology to politics. For a long period he conducted the local preachers' column in Hughes's *Methodist Times*. A life-long abstainer, there was no more effective advocate of total abstinence in the country. His holidays were spent in ardent mountaineering. As a journalist once said of him, 'he was as much at home in the peaceful atmosphere of a snowstorm on one of the Alpine giants as he was in the warmer atmosphere of party politics'. His wife, formerly Miss Bretherton, shared his enthusiasm, and also conquered with her axe some of the peaks of the Oberland and Engadine.

Bamford Slack served for a long period on the General Committee, and was elected President in 1894 after only twelve years' membership of the Association and nine of the General Committee. He was the youngest President ever elected. For many years the General Committee met at his home in Woburn Square, London, during 'Cattle Show Week'. On at least one occasion they were addressed there by Hugh Price Hughes. In 1902 the Aggregate Meeting elected him as its Honorary Secretary, which office he held for three years. He was also a Trustee. He died at Woburn Square in 1909 when in the full tide of his active life.

Another lawyer of distinction, Sir George Royle, C.B.E., J.P., F.C.I.I., of Bedford, was President in 1908. Happily, he is still with us. A barrister-at-law, and Fellow of the Royal Geographical Society, during his active career he had chambers in the Middle Temple. Yet it was not until his son decided to become a solicitor that Sir George himself began to study law. He was called to the Bar at the Middle Temple in 1905. He had already achieved success in the world of Insurance. He went on to a systematic study of legal problems, accomplishing his aim by means of orderly methods and a most retentive and well-trained memory. He did not diminish his work either as a preacher or in local government. Indeed, he also accepted the office of Mayor of Bedford, and on April 28th, 1944, was made a Freeman of the Borough, in recognition and appreciation of fifty years' public service. Sir George in his heyday was a preacher of remarkable ability. A wide reader and an original thinker, impassioned and challenging in his pulpit and platform style, he could hold large crowds and win the conviction of his hearers. The Kingdom of God and the cause of the Mutual Aid were magnificently served by this unconventional and learned advocate. Until retirement in 1944, for more than thirty years he was Chairman of the Bedfordshire Insurance Committee, and for a similar period a member of the National Savings Committee. His character was radiant and his humour never-failing.

Very different in temperament was Stephen R. Dodds, who became President in 1940. Also a lawyer, his strength lay in a quiet, patient, tolerant, and always understanding appreciation. He held tenaciously to firm views both in politics and religion. His outlook was modern and soundly informed. Exuberance was foreign to his nature. But he could express his views with great clarity, and he was courageous both in the pulpit and in his Mutual Aid leadership. He came late into the work of the Association but soon held a position of authority within its inner Cabinet. His death deprived the movement of a leader it could ill afford to lose. Never spectacular, he sought neither office nor distinction, but did not shirk the responsibilities when both were thrust upon him. His great gifts of mind and heart were devoted without reserve to the service of his less fortunate fellow preachers.

A. J. Cash, of Derby, also a 'man of the law', shrewd and successful, was a leading layman before Union of the United Methodist Church. The Nottingham Aggregate of 1919 elected him as President. He had become a local preacher in 1890 at the age of 17, and joined the Association in the following year. His value was soon appreciated in his Circuit and District, and in 1906 he was elected to the General Committee. A convinced Free Churchman, he was for three years President of the Derbyshire Federation of Free Church Councils. Temperance and the Sunday schools also had in him a keen worker. His conviction that the Methodist Churches should come together in one consolidated witness led him to take a notable part in the accomplishing of Methodist Union, of which he may be described as one of the legal architects. For many years his firm was the Association's official legal adviser. Reserved and unflurried in manner, he did not wear his heart on his sleeve; indeed, at times in debate his attitude might seem dry and pedantic. But he was ever actuated by a profound, if dissembled, love of his fellows, and no trouble was too much for him to take in the interests of the Association.

A contrast to these gentlemen 'of light and learning' is William Stoker, the friend of George Jacob Holyoake, pioneer of the Co-operative movement. Born in 1834 in the colliery village of Burradon in Northumberland, he was a member of a large and economically poor family. All the boys had to go early to the pit; indeed, he was fortunate who did not go before he was 10. Having to work for twelve to fourteen hours a day, he had little leisure-time for study. Yet study he did. He loved books, and built up a library of several thousands of well-thumbed volumes. His range was not narrow, and he became familiar with the intricacies of industrial, social, political, scientific, and theological subjects. After his early conversion he joined the United Methodist Free Church at Blyth, and was soon its secretary.

Discerning preachers saw in him a most promising recruit, and they were not disappointed. Soon congregations were flocking to hear him, and Holyoake himself was among his most eager listeners. One of the earliest members of the Seaton Delaval Co-operative Society, he was its Treasurer for twenty years; and his abilities were such that he was elected a director of the Co-operative Wholesale Society, in whose interests he travelled extensively in Europe, America, and Australia. He was politically an advanced Radical. He did much to help the miners of Northumberland and Durham, and encouraged the establishment of the miners' institutes which in his day had so important a part in adult education. As a public debater his renown spread far and wide. Throughout his active life, however, preaching remained his first concern, and he was a doughty Mutual Aid champion. He died in 1903, having been taken suddenly ill while attending to public duties in Manchester.

Joseph Wardle, born in 1839 amid the majestic peaks of Derbyshire, near the rise of the River Dove, was the son of a labourer and went to work at 12 years of age. At 16 he stood for hiring in the Longnor Market and was engaged by a farmer at £6 a year! He had scanty education, but great natural gifts. His sister Mary married a distant relative of Dr. Jabez Bunting, and he held that it was in answer to her prayers that as a lad he was converted in a tiny Primitive Methodist chapel. He at once joined a class that met in the house of his grandmother—she had been alive in John Wesley's day. Soon several of his companions also gave themselves to God. The class of eleven became twenty-five. He began first to serve in the Sunday school, and later was invited to preach, coming on the Plan in 1863. In winter he frequently trudged ten miles through snow to keep his appointments.

In 1885 he gave up his country work to become a lay agent of the Manchester Mission. There he became the friend of General Gordon, who had been sent by the Government to Manchester as an engineer on work concerning the city boundary. Gordon, whose profound Christian experience always sought practical expression, went to the office of the Mission and asked to be allowed to accompany one of the agents as he worked around his district. Wardle took him into the poorest areas, showed him how the people were having to live, and introduced him to the Mission's redemptive work. Gordon was vastly impressed, and often went sick-visiting with his new-found friend and supported him at open-air meetings and in Ragged School work. They also held services in the tramps' wards from half-past ten to half-past eleven at night, preaching the Gospel to drunkards and prostitutes. The friendship thus begun was continued to the day of Gordon's death at Khartoum.

A breakdown in health compelled Joseph Wardle to retire from the exacting work of the Mission and for forty-two years he served the Prudential Insurance Company. But preaching was still his vocation. He travelled over 50,000 miles, visiting America, Canada, France, Palestine, Egypt, Italy, Switzerland, and Germany, proclaiming the evangel wherever he went. He was an indefatigable cyclist, and in five years cycled over twenty thousand miles on preaching service. He also wrote several books, including *General Gordon: Saint and Soldier*, which had a vogue in its day.

Among the Association's stormy petrels must be numbered 'Gourley of Gateshead'. Powerful in debate, A. Gourley was ever the sworn foe of complacency. He specialized in attacks upon self-satisfied Aggregate Meeting platform officials. Sometimes in mid-afternoon on a warm June day the atmosphere would become a little drowsy, and then it was that he would launch his thunderbolts. His strident North-country voice would penetrate to the remotest corner of the conference chapel, with something of the effect of an electric storm. As a commentator once wrote, that voice was 'a tocsin, a summons to battle, or, at least, the signal for a row'. He thrived on such wordy warfare. His tall, ungainly, grey-haired figure would dominate the assembly by its rugged vigour and utter, passionate sincerity. Clad in the familiar frock-coat in which he always preached on Sundays, in his lapel invariably and defiantly the blue-

and-white ribbon of abstinence, he was fearless, blunt, and uncompromising. He could on occasion be cantankerous. He could intervene in a debate and sweep away opposition by the sheer force of his rhetoric. Formidable as an antagonist, he was not always appreciated by those whose cause he espoused; they were apt to murmur a prayer to be saved from the extravagances of their friend. The Graces certainly did not attend his cradle. Yet he was indefatigable in his efforts to advance the work of the Association in his own Circuit and District, and if he believed in hitting hard he could take hard knocks in return with good humour. 'F. H. B.' once sketched him thus: 'Open the chestnut-burs of his rough and prickly exterior, and you shall find a heart of gold, and great goodwill, and much love for his fellows.'

To turn to Moses Atkinson is to enter another world. It says much for any movement that it could hold the allegiance of such strangely different men. Born at Leeds in 1848 and educated at the Grammar School there, he was of independent means and gave his whole life to preaching. He was essentially a bookman, gracious, cultured, far-seeing. But he also knew men, and how to attract them to his Master. His wise counsel, deep insight, and persuasive advocacy placed him in the foremost rank of the Association's statesmen. There was much that he might have done—for example, in politics; but he preferred to serve the Church. He was one of the small band of men who persuaded the Wesleyan Conference to establish a Department of the Church to promote and safeguard the interests of local preachers, and he was the first Treasurer of the Connexional Committee. He became a member of the Association's General Committee at Manchester in

1884, and was President in 1886—an unprecedentedly swift advance. He was never content, however, to bask in Connexional limelight: he did solid work in comparative obscurity for many years as a District Convenor, ever patient, painstaking, and methodical. He died, as he had lived, in the service of the Church. In July 1917 he went to Manchester for a Mutual Aid week-end. On the Sunday morning he conducted the service in Gravel Lane Chapel. In the night he was taken suddenly unwell, and died at his host's house in the early hours of Monday.

Sir John Barnsley, who came to the Chair in the Jubilee Year, 1899, was another aristocrat of the movement, who, having entered into a goodly personal inheritance, spent himself in Mutual Aid work. Educated at King Edward's Grammar School in Birmingham, he was the worthy son of a fine old class-leader and a mother of deep piety and marked individuality. He began to preach at 18 and taught for many years in the Islington School, as well as conducting an Adult Bible Class with an average attendance of 1,200. He entered the family business of John Barnsley and Sons, builders and contractors, and gave splendid service in the public life of Birmingham. A polished and eloquent speaker, of soldierly appearance and winsome personality, with a beautiful platform voice and great charm of manner, he was aptly described as 'a prince of preachers and platform orators'. He was one of the Connexional Secretaries of the Twentieth Century Fund, and served for ten years on the L.P.M.A. General Committee.

These are but a few of the fathers to whom the movement owes its very existence. What more could be written, if there were space, of many other illustrious pioneers—of John Dickenson, the Bradford blacksmith who gave himself for forty years to work among the 'down-and-out' in slum and prison; of Joseph Hewertson, the village blacksmith of Windermere, at whose smithy John Ruskin often paused for a chat, who loved simple things and preached with great natural ability; of Enoch Morris of Ashby-de-la-Zouch, who learned to ride a bicycle at 67, rode it several miles every day when over eighty, and cycled 4,840 miles to preach, carrying his dinner in his pocket and eating it by the wayside between appointments; of Charles Heap, J.P., who retired from the Wesleyan ministry to take hold of the business in Rochdale when his father died, gave great benefactions to that town, became the Association's Treasurer, and President in 1896 when it was struggling for a place in the Connexional sun; of Osmond Ogier Noel of Southport, President in 1913, a Guernsey man who built up a successful business as a cotton-spinner in Lancashire, rugged, humorous, passionate, formidable in debate; of Sir George Lunn, Lord Mayor of Newcastle, who, when King George the Fifth, on an extended visit to the city, asked him after resting for a while how he had rested, replied: 'By taking my appointment at one of our smaller churches'; of Major-General A. H. E. Campbell, son of a Judge of the Madras High Court and himself Judge in the Suburban Court of Judicature of Hyderabad, India, and close friend of the Nizam, who became a local preacher after meeting the Rev. William Burgess out East, and eventually settling in Sheffield lived to be 94; of Harry and Tilden Bisseker, both Presidents, men of mystical experience and culture; of Page Woodcock, journalist and lecturer, 'Uncle Reg' of the *Sunday Circle;* of J. H. Freeborough, of strong Liberal convictions, an unbending Wesleyan Reformer, a preacher steeped in Chalmers,

Denny, Bruce, and Barth, unhumorous but great-hearted, three times President of the Wesleyan Reform Union and a powerful influence in the life of Sheffield and the West Riding; and of Howell Mabbott, Celt and Cornishman, witty, charming, passionately sincere, who came to the Presidency in Quaker Darlington, and for many years was called upon when the Association wished to express worthily its appreciation of the welcome offered by dignitaries of Church and State! These all served in faith, adorning the movement with their richly various personalities and gifts.

CHAPTER FIVE

THE SUCCESSION CONTINUES

FINALLY, a group of men who may be said to have shaped the Association's course during the present century. The first of them, John Harding, was born in the East Riding of Yorkshire into a family that had farmed land in the neighbourhood of Danby Wiske, Northallerton, for nearly four hundred years. He was essentially a Yorkshireman, blunt, dependable, sagacious. Soon after his conversion he began to speak in farm kitchens and at cottage services. He conducted his first service in a village chapel at the age of 17. As a preacher he was 'pointed, plain, but by no means commonplace', and during his long career he preached in more than six hundred chapels. He was the General Secretary of the Association for thirty-one years, until his death in 1914, and proved himself to be a master of detail as well as an official whose warm human sympathy, though kept in check by a cool and businesslike head, was always at the service of his needy brethren. Never showy, he refused the limelight; but the work owes much to his unfailing devotion.

W. J. Back, to whom reference has already been made, was President in 1914. A man of Devon, born at Exeter in 1860, he was converted at the Mint Chapel in that city. He moved to London at the age of 21, and immersed himself in good works, of which he regarded preaching as his chief vocation. At Warwick Gardens Wesleyan

Church he taught in the Sunday school of which later he became Superintendent, and also led a class. He rendered great service to the Association for a long period as its Organizing Secretary, working in close co-operation with John Harding. Masterful in personality, he was never one to suffer fools gladly, but he gave all his powers to preaching and Mutual Aid affairs. His shrewd judgement, tenacious character, and West Country eloquence, made him invaluable in the strategic work of the movement. Honorary Secretary 1904-26, he inaugurated the Convenors' breakfast in 1906. The measure of his successful work may be judged from the fact that of the £450,000 disbursed by the Association up to 1927, when he died, £200,000 had been distributed in the last fifteen years.

Another justly famed leader was W. E. Skinner, who became one of the Honorary Secretaries in 1904 and served in that office until his death in 1921. He was born at Hackney, London, in 1853, with no advantages other than his native gifts. He had to go out to work at the age of 11. But, determined to improve his position, he attended evening classes, studied hard, and especially mastered scientific subjects. So successful was he that in 1870, with the turn of the tide in English education, he was accepted as a pupil teacher at Radnor Street Wesleyan Day School in East London. Four years later he was appointed assistant master at Wilmot Street Board School, Bethnal Green. In 1875 he passed his certificate examination and during the next thirteen years served first as headmaster of a temporary Board School at Bonnar Lane, Bethnal Green, and then as second master at Cranbrook Road.

His love of books led him to think of writing about them in the religious newspapers. He sent reviews to the

Methodist Times, and Hugh Price Hughes printed them. Then he was asked to report Methodist meetings. He found that he had a ready pen and a flair for journalism. Hughes became increasingly interested in him, and conducted his wedding service. In 1888 there came the opportunity to join the staff of the *Methodist Recorder* as a sub-editor under the editorship of Nehemiah Curnock, and he at once gave up teaching and devoted himself wholly to Fleet Street. There his painstaking devotion to detail made him a dependable, indeed invaluable, member of the staff. Never flurried, he was a good proof-reader, and if not brilliant in ideas could be relied upon to watch over the interests of the paper and shape adequately even the most unlikely 'copy'.

It was aptly said of him that his religion was not emotional but steady, deep, and practical. Thoughtful and impressive as a preacher, he was in counsel a statesman. Exact and conscientious, he would take the utmost care over what might at times, to others, seem trivial details; but those who worked with him best appreciated his sterling qualities. For a while he was a member of James Smetham's society class at Stoke Newington. He was elected to the General Committee in 1888 and became President in 1902. For many years he wrote the Annual Report, and read to the Committee the draft of the last one to come from his pen only thirteen days before he died in April 1921. In his memory a stone was erected by fellow-members of the Association in Ilford cemetery.

Sir William H. Stephenson, four times Mayor and thrice Lord Mayor of Newcastle-upon-Tyne, was one of the most remarkable men who ever came from Tyneside.

Born six miles from the city in 1836, he was proud

to claim Methodist ancestry back to the days of John Wesley. He used to refer to the entry in the *Journal* for 7th December 1742: 'I was so ill in the morning that I was obliged to send Mr. Williams to the Room. He afterwards went to Mr. Stephenson, a merchant in the town, who had a passage through the ground we intended to buy. I was willing to purchase it. Mr. Stephenson told him: "Sir, I do not want money; but if Mr. Wesley wants ground, he may have a piece of my garden, adjoining to the place you mention. . . . For forty pounds he shall have sixteen yards in breadth and thirty in length." ' And on Wednesday 8th December: 'Mr. Stephenson and I signed an article, and I took possession of the ground.' On that ground still stands Wesley's 'Orphan House', near the Brunswick Chapel. The merchant mentioned in the *Journal* was Sir William Stephenson's great grandfather. His parents held services in their house for twenty-five years before the chapel was built in the village. They also jointly led a society class, Mr. Stephenson leading the men and his wife the women. Thus the boy was brought up in the atmosphere of Methodist piety.

He was sent to school at Wesley College, Sheffield, under the Principalship of Dr. Samuel D. Waddy. While he was there a revival broke out in the school, and it influenced his whole life. At 17 he entered his father's business, and in due time succeeded to its control. Gradually he extended its scope, and his enterprise gave him leadership in many commercial undertakings in the worlds of shipping, gas, insurance, and metal-work. Finally, he achieved a leading post on the Tyne Commission which developed a shallow stream into a highway of commerce on which could float battleships and great liners. He was appointed Chairman in 1900, and held the office until his death. It would not be possible to exaggerate the part he played in bringing prosperity to his native city.

Nevertheless, his commercial interests, great as they were, absorbed only a fraction of his energies. Deeply concerned for the welfare of his fellows, he plunged into the problems of local government, entered the City Council in 1869, and within six years was elected Mayor. This high office he filled on three other occasions, and when it was raised to the dignity of a Lord Mayoralty he again presided over the city for three years in succession. In 1911 the city acknowledged his devoted service by electing him an Honorary Freeman. Meanwhile, in 1900, he had been knighted by Queen Victoria. Three years later he presented to Newcastle a statue of the Queen by Sir Alfred Gilbert, R.A.

Ever keen to promote education, he gave three public libraries—at Elswick, Heaton, and Walker. His benefactions to Newcastle Methodism were too numerous for detailed mention here; they included several churches, church-halls, and manses. He started to preach at 23, and soon became a keen worker for the Mutual Aid and a member of the General Committee. He was one of the few who twice occupied the Chair, and on both occasions at Newcastle-upon-Tyne—in 1883 and 1895. When the Jubilee of the Association was celebrated in 1899 he launched, with a noble gift, the 'Sir W. H. Stephenson Jubilee Widows' Fund'. One of the most distinguished public men who have actively supported the Mutual Aid, he died in 1918 after a life devoted to the service of his fellow-men.

Among the unusual personalities who have left their mark upon the Association none has been more widely respected than Sir Thomas Rowbotham, of Stockport. Born in Cheshire in 1851, he was at the age of 13 apprenticed to a village blacksmith, and worked at the anvil for twenty years. His conversion, and introduction to Methodism, was due to the zeal of an obscure but faithful Methodist whom he providentially met on the Saturday he arrived in the village. Invited to go with him to the 'band meeting', the boy went, expecting to hear a programme of music. But the music turned out to be lively Methodist hymns, interspersed with definite, and very pointed, prayers. One of the old saints mentioned Thomas Rowbotham to God in his prayer! That made a deep impression upon the lad's heart. The very next day he joined the Sunday school, and a year later, following the appeal of a local preacher from the adjoining circuit of New Mills, he gave himself to Christ in the little chapel at Gee Cross, Hyde Circuit. Not long afterwards the appointed preacher failed to appear and one of the Sunday school teachers conducted the afternoon service. To the boy's surprise, he asked Tom to preach in the evening, and preach he did, taking as his text the question of the Philippian gaoler, 'What must I do to be saved?' At 17 Thomas Rowbotham was admitted to the full Plan.

He had few opportunities of study. During his apprenticeship his master gave him food and lodgings and clothing—and 3*d.* a week to spend! He gave two-thirds of that to the church. He had to begin work at six o'clock in the morning and did not finish until eight in the evening. But soon he formed the habit of rising at five o'clock to read and study. He tackled such books as Watson's *Institutes*, Watts on *The Mind*, and Locke's *Essay Concerning Human Understanding*. He read all the biographical and theological books he could borrow. Soon he began to think of moving out into a wider world, but he was 34 when the chance came. He got a job as a commercial traveller, and moved to Stockport, where he began his great work at the famous Trinity Church.

It was while travelling that his observations in South Wales led him to see the need for a self-oiling train wheel and axle. He strove to make one, and at last, through dogged persistence, succeeded, and having patented it, launched it successfully upon the commercial market. From that moment his business success was assured. He began to take an interest in the municipal affairs of Stockport, becoming a member of the Council, a magistrate, and Mayor. For a long period he was Chairman of the Licensing Bench. When the Broadstone Mills Ltd., in which hundreds of Stockport people had invested their savings, was threatened with ruin, he saved the situation by guaranteeing its finances at the bank. He then became its Chairman and by shrewd and skilful direction turned defeat into triumph. He was knighted in 1920.

Success did not spoil him. Wealth made no difference to his genial, friendly temperament. He remained a simple and fervent Methodist who rejoiced in preaching and served on the General Committee of the Mutual Aid Association and as President in 1909-10. All through his life he delighted in Lancashire poetry, and in his racy addresses, which were always liberally spiced with humour, he frequently referred to Edwin Waugh and other Lancashire writers. He loved to recall that at the first Christmas party after he joined the Methodists at Gee Cross, he recited some verses by the Lancashire dialect writer, Sam Laycock, the first lines of which were:

Between these shoe soles an' this hat
Stands a very respectable mon;
Neaow there's nobody'ull contradict that,
An' why? Becose nobody con.

He used to pause, and smile, and say: 'Not bad for a lad of 13.' His many generous gifts to the town of Stockport included Woodbank Hall in its lovely park and its woods beside the River Goyt, with wonderful views of the hills of Cheshire and Derbyshire. He also provided an infirmary and a convalescent home. Generosity was the keynote of his mind. Rugged, masterful, by some standards unpolished, he had the culture of one to whom the Bible was an open book, and a never-failing kindliness of heart.

In his New Year message to the Magazine during his Presidential year he used words that may with profit be recalled forty years after:

> I believe it to be absolutely essential to maintain the lay element among our preachers, and that every pulpit from which the lay element is excluded suffers a distinct loss. And let us not forget that our work as preachers is the salvation of the individual, that no social or political reforms can take the place of repentance toward God and faith in our Lord Jesus Christ—that the first requisite is a clean heart and a right spirit, and that for these men must find their way to the Cross; that if social order must be just, men must be made just.

Arthur Cowling represented quite a different school of Methodist thought. His mind, that of a trained schoolmaster, was essentially modern. So much so, indeed, that those of his brethren who delight in choosing labels were apt to describe him as 'a modernist'. In so far as the phrase indicates a readiness to apprehend the new truths that are for ever breaking out from the Word, it was apt; in so far as it implied a lack of evangelical zeal it was wholly inappropriate.

He was cradled and nurtured in Yorkshire—at Pateley Bridge. His parents were working folk, and he was sent as a child to be a half-timer in a bobbin factory. From 12 to 17 he worked full time in the mill. So keen was he to get on, however, that he worked in a blacksmith's shop in the little spare time that was his so as to earn money to buy books. His persistence was rewarded. He passed the necessary examinations and became a schoolmaster. Ultimately he became Headmaster of Wigan Wesleyan Day School, from which he retired in 1927. As a speaker he could be brilliant. His words were always challenging. He was no respecter of persons. Intensely sincere, his vision was clear and burning; he could stab the most slumbrous audience wide awake. Tall, slim, pale, fidgety and restless on a platform or in a pulpit, he not only sparkled as a public speaker but also had a grasp of detail that fitted him for the exacting work of Honorary Secretary, the duties of which he carried out with conspicuous success. Elected to the Chair at Bristol in 1922, he was one of the Association's greatest Presidents. His death from a sudden heart attack a fortnight after the Aggregate Meeting of 1930 was a sad loss to the movement.

Mention must be made of genial, dapper, friendly William H. Thornton, J.P., President at Plymouth in 1931. A 'man of Kent', he was born at Gillingham on the right bank of the Medway, the son of a devoted local preacher in the Rochester Circuit. He and F. H. Buss were on the same circuit plan as young men, and remained lifelong, intimate friends. It was W. H. Thornton who invited F. H. Buss to his first Aggregate and he and his father heard his trial sermon at Rochester. Years later he inducted F. H. B. into the Chair. His spruce, energetic figure, good-humoured features, and pointed beard were well known throughout English Methodism. No one would describe him as shy or retiring, but his evident self-confidence was friendly, humorous, and rooted in service for others. He was a hard worker with warm pastoral gifts rather than an orator or a leader. He served his town and his Church with unqualified enthusiasm, and was tireless in good deeds. He died suddenly in 1939 while chatting with his doctor.

H. G. Hunt brought many quiet gifts to the Association's service. A newspaper man, he had served on the business and circulation side of daily papers in Bradford, Dublin, and Sheffield before coming to London as Manager of the *Methodist Times* when Mr. J. Arthur Rank acquired it. He was born at Birmingham and became a local preacher as a young man under the influence of Luke Wiseman in the Birmingham Mission. At Bradford he became acquainted with W. Riley, the author, and the friendship continued, and deepened, until his death. He served for several terms on the General Committee and was the Aggregate Meeting Journal Secretary. A wide and deep reader, he was a preacher of choice spirit and careful diction; he held large congregations under a spell. As circuit steward for his friend the Rev. George McNeal he did much to recreate the influence of Wesley's Chapel, London, as a Methodist shrine. He collapsed soon after returning from the Aggregate Meeting in Reading in 1942, and died at Henley-in-Arden, where he lies buried in the Garden of England.

Arthur Gregory, President in 1937, was a valued friend of William Temple, Archbishop of Canterbury. They met at Aldershot, when Gregory was Headmaster of the West End Boys' School, and co-operated in good works. The relationship continued, and Gregory was present by invitation in Canterbury Cathedral when Temple was enthroned in the Chair of St. Augustine. After the service the Archbishop sent a message asking him to come to his room, and there the two men spoke together of the things that lay deepest in their hearts Born at. Wolverhampton, Arthur Gregory was trained at Westminster Training College. Throughout his career he exercised a great influence. To him boys were always individuals. Out of school hours he would take them for rambles and thus introduce them to the fascinating study of nature. He was also a keen exponent of adult education and advocated far and near the aims of the Workers' Educational Association. After a long life of active service he retired to his native town, rejoined Trinity Church which he had attended in youth, and led a weekly fellowship class. His gifts both as speaker and writer were ever at the service of the Association, and always he sought opportunities for evangelism. Great-hearted, he was also intellectually adventurous, and to the end retained his wide human sympathies.

During the last thirty years, it may be said, three men emerged into the vanguard of leadership within the Association. One of them, R. Parkinson Tomlinson—'Parkie' to his friends—died unexpectedly on the eve of the 1943 Aggregate Meeting, shortly after preaching his last sermon, during his second term as President. He was elected to that high office at Lincoln in 1928, and again in 1942 at Reading.

He was the grandson of Thomas Tomlinson, a local preacher, and the son of William Tomlinson who, although not a preacher, held many influential offices in the Methodist Church at Poulton-le-Fylde in Lancashire. The boy was thus cradled in Methodism. It is not to be wondered at that he began to preach before he was 20. His gifts were such that before long he was in great demand for special services. He joined his father in his corn-merchant's business, and plunged into the life of the busy Garstang Circuit, preaching, organizing debt-cancelling efforts, and championing circuit claims in the forum of the Liverpool Synod. As Sunday school teacher, class leader, circuit steward, member of the Urban District Council, several times its Chairman, and eventually as Liberal Member of Parliament for Lancaster, succeeding Sir Norval Helme, another Methodist, who represented the Division for eighteen years—in all these and many other ways he gave of his best. Never marrying, he was able to devote his entire life unreservedly to business and his Church. In 1938 the Methodist Conference made him its Vice-President.

His gay, debonair, friendly personality endeared him to the whole Association. In 1930 he succeeded Arthur Cowling as Honorary Secretary, and thus began an ideal partnership in that office with F. Harold Buss. The two made a perfect team. Parkinson Tomlinson especially concerned himself with the devotional side of the Aggregate Meeting, and it was always a moving experience when, at the opening of a session, he read from the Scriptures in that natural, dramatic way of his. As a preacher, he was ever passionately evangelical. His travels over many parts of the world and his wide knowledge of men and affairs contributed to the appeal of his sermons and addresses. He could move great crowds, and was popular as a speaker at brotherhoods and Central Halls. His love for his Lord overflowed into a love for his fellow men, which was especially manifest in his ceaseless labours for aged and broken preachers. It will be long before the influence of his dynamic personality ceases to be felt.

It has been decided that, as a general rule, there shall be no reference in this history of the Association to officials who are still living. The record, however, would not be complete without some mention of two men to whom the movement has owed more during the last half-century than to any others—F. Harold Buss and William Ewart Noddings.

Harold Buss was born at Farncombe in Surrey in 1876, of Cornish ancestry on his mother's side. Six years later the family settled at Chatham and became members of Bethel Wesleyan Church, Rochester. Educated at Sir Joseph Williamson's Mathematical School, Rochester, he entered the Civil Service, to which he gave the active years of his career. He began to preach when he was 19, was admitted to full plan in 1898. In 1906 he married the daughter of Major Charles Waldron, of the Royal Engineers, and moved to Herne Hill, in the Mostyn Road Circuit, London, and for twenty years F. H. B. shared in the leadership of the society.

The work of the Mutual Aid Association early kindled his imagination and enlisted his sympathies, and before long he was advocating its claims in pulpit and church courts. In 1912 he was elected to the General Committee, five years later became Joint Editor of the Magazine, and from 1921 to 1926 was its sole Editor. In that year, on the death of Arthur Cowling, he was called to the high office of Honorary Secretary, thus fulfilling the expectations of those elder statesmen of the Association who had recognized in him the qualities that are necessary for supreme leadership. When in 1932 he was elected President, the Association rightly felt that in all its history there had been no more worthy appointment, and when the time came to nominate the Centenary President only one name was regarded as appropriate—that of F. Harold Buss.

For at least thirty years his gracious, courteous, yet strong personality has exercised a determining influence within the movement. He has given the best of his many good qualities to its service. The Magazine has been enriched by his skilful, allusive pen; 'Obiter Dicta' will ever be associated with his initials. Firmly Liberal in politics, his pungently expressed opinions have at times upset the traditionalists on the one hand and the Leftists on the other; but all have united in appreciation of his sincerity and fairmindedness. At the Aggregate Meeting and in the General Committee he has displayed considerable powers as a tactician, shrewdly knowing when to rebuke, yet ever lavish in praise. There have been occasions when the working of his complex mind has left his brethren wondering just what he really wanted to do, but on the whole his statesmanship has been farseeing and generous. Modest without pretence, an accomplished and witty speaker, a bookman whose love of George Meredith places him among the elect, a man of wide culture and unfailing kindliness, he has indeed been a great gift of God to the Association. He has done much to ensure for it wise and reticent guidance during a period when its immense success brought it into disturbed waters, and to set the goodly ship firmly upon a fair course for its second century.

There are Gladstonian qualities in William Ewart Noddings, who from 1914 to 1946 as General Secretary did much to consolidate and extend the Association's work. He gave to it the undivided loyalty of a trained and systematic business mind and a heart of sympathy and love. No official has ever been more expert in his management of the affairs of Head Office. He came with the experience of nineteen years in the service of the Seaton Carew Iron Company, Ltd., as the paymaster of some seven hundred and fifty men, and his mastery of insurance, compensation, and similar schemes enabled him quickly to grasp the details of the by no means simple administrative problems that faced the Association in an era of social progress. Through two world wars, and the uneasy armistice between them, a period of unrest and economic strain, he upheld the traditions of the movement and maintained and even extended its beneficent work.

Shrewd, unflurried, not easily taken in, he nevertheless always approached the day-to-day routine with pity for the hard-pressed and a keen sense of human values. The 'cases' he brought to the attention of the General Committee were never merely 'cases' to him: they were men and women in distress for whom Christ died. Thus his administration was not formal. He wrote to annuitants and applicants not just as an official seeking information required for the files, but as a brother in Christ seeking to help in a time of difficulty. Precise, efficient, scrupulous he invariably was, but also understanding of human foibles, responsive to sensitiveness, human and adaptable and overflowing with tenderness.

As a preacher also W. E. Noddings has exceptional qualities. The intensity of his deep convictions moves his congregations to respond. A student, he has great resources; a class-leader, he knows how to handle thinking men; a deep reader, he is well-equipped in Methodist theology; imaginative and sensitive, he can with burning words evoke from others the passionate sincerity kindled in his own soul. In the North, in Clapham, and latterly in Weybridge, he has given to local Methodism the full service of heart and mind; and in every county of England and Wales he has proclaimed with great acceptance as an L.P.M.A. evangelist the unsearchable riches of Christ.

APPENDIX

THE PLACES WHERE THE ANNUAL MEETINGS HAVE BEEN HELD, AND THE NAMES OF PRESIDENTS.

YEAR	PLACE	PRESIDENT	DIED	AGE
1849	London	Wm. Harris	13th June 1900	87
1850	Birmingham	Isaac English	23rd November 1855	61
1851	Sheffield	W. B. Carter	10th June 1887	85
1852	Huddersfield	William Nelstrop	10th September 1877	76
1853	Leeds	John Unwin	15th December 1895	84
1854	London	James Wild	1st May 1866	83
1855	Bristol	Richard Carter	1st December 1884	79
1856	Sheffield	Thos. Chamberlain	27th March 1889	70
1857	Louth	J. B. Sharpley	24th June 1872	72
1858	Birmingham	John Towne	3rd December 1887	87
1859	Norwich	Josh. Massingham	22nd February 1868	58
1860	London	Thos. Cuthbertson	26th September 1875	61
1861	Bath	John Wade	24th April 1890	88
1862	Derby	Thomas Hirst	30th June 1870	81
1863	Manchester	James Arundale	15th July 1886	76
1864	London	Richard Durley	16th January 1888	89
1865	Norwich	John Carter	31st December 1908	97
1866	Sheffield	Thomas Cole	8th November 1902	78
1867	York	David Hill	22nd August 1876	67
1868	Ashton-under-Lyne	George Thompson	12th August 1884	74
1869	London	William Bowron	30th November 1890	80
1870	Northampton	S. D. Waddy	24th December 1902	72
1871	Keighley	N. A. Aldersley	19th October 1899	73
1872	Louth	Wm. Jameson	26th February 1886	75
1873	Norwich	Robert Daws	3rd November 1892	67
1874	Manchester	Abraham Andrew	17th January 1889	70
1875	London	W. W. Pocock	18th September 1899	85
1876	Cardiff	Dr. Aldom	29th August 1885	64
1877	Lynn	Edwin Benson	17th February 1886	74
1878	Hull	Ald. Dowsing	25th August 1882	62
1879	Oldham	Joseph Milsom	14th April 1899	78
1880	York	C. S. Madder	20th November 1909	82
1881	Sheffield	S. M. Johnson	29th November 1925	85
1882	Leicester	J. Dyson	26th February 1895	81
1883	Newcastle-on-Tyne	Sir W. H. Stephenson	7th May 1918	82
1884	Manchester	A. R. Johnson	31st March 1902	61
1885	London	G. C. Amphlett	1st July 1898	68
1886	Leeds	M. Atkinson	2nd July 1917	69
1887	Liverpool	J. W. Laycock	6th May 1923	87
1888	Nottingham	William Kilner	17th August 1893	67
1889	Bradford	S. Rathbone Edge	27th September 1930	88
1890	Birmingham	W. O. Clough	2nd May, 1922	76
1891	York	George Luckley	11th December 1911	86
1892	Bristol	Jas. Calvert Coates	16th June 1911	73
1893	Hull	Hugh Wyatt	24th November 1914	73
1894	Burslem	Sir J. Bamford Slack	11th February 1909	51
1895	Newcastle-on-Tyne	Sir W. H. Stephenson	7th May 1918	82

THE PLACES WHERE THE ANNUAL MEETINGS HAVE BEEN HELD, AND THE NAMES OF PRESIDENTS.

YEAR	PLACE	PRESIDENT	DIED	AGE
1896	Bolton	Charles Heap	24th July 1923	78
1897	Plymouth	J. W. Walker	7th September 1939	91
1898	Manchester	John Broxap	30th January 1913	76
1899	Birmingham	B.-Gen. Sir J. Barnsley	19th January 1926	67
1900	Sheffield	H. Emmerson	18th January 1915	62
1901	Liverpool	Thomas Snape	9th August 1912	76
1902	London	W. E. Skinner	22nd April 1921	67
1903	Leeds	George Crossfield	27th March 1919	81
1904	Nottingham	Sir Wm. Smith	12th January 1916	72
1905	York	Wm. Butterworth	19th April 1914	63
1906	Bradford	David Barr	9th March 1910	79
1907	Bristol	B. G. Berry	23rd April 1921	79
1908	Hull	Sir George Royle		
1909	Hanley	Sir Thos. Rowbotham	October 1939	88
1910	Newcastle-on-Tyne	J. T. Burden	1st August 1926	72
1911	Bolton	Tilden J. Bisseker	12th January 1940	88
1912	Birmingham	W. H. Jennings	19th October 1917	70
1913	Manchester	O. O. Noel	6th June 1939	82
1914	Sheffield	W. J. Back	6th November 1927	66
1915	Plymouth	R. Lindley	2nd July 1935	75
1916	Liverpool	H. Bisseker	11th September 1940	86
1917	London	W. Greenhalgh	23rd May 1921	69
1918	Leeds	J. W. Hampson	14th August 1927	68
1919	Nottingham	A. J. Cash	13th May 1944	71
1920	Darlington	Howell Mabbott	9th February 1943	84
1921	Bradford	W. Douthwaite		
1922	Bristol	A. Cowling	23rd June 1930	62
1923	Hull	E. R. Lightwood	2nd February 1933	
1924	Bolton	Henry Ball	10th May 1925	68
1925	Newcastle-on-Tyne	T. E. Nuttall	21st October 1928	68
1926	Hanley	J. Simpson Alcock	16th October 1936	78
1927	Birmingham	S. Smethurst	3rd February 1931	78
1928	Lincoln	R. P. Tomlinson	3rd June 1943	62
1929	Bournemouth	Harry Dawson		
1930	Manchester	J. P. Williams	3rd March 1942	78
1931	Plymouth	W. H. Thornton	23rd July 1939	74
1932	Sheffield	F. Harold Buss		
1933	Liverpool	Walter Kirkham		
1934	Leeds	Charles Hart	26th February 1948	78
1935	London	W. J. Johns		
1936	Nottingham	Fred Ogden		
1937	Cardiff	Arthur Gregory	6th September 1947	84
1938	London	James Morgan		
1939	Bradford	R. J. Soper		
1940	Bolton	Stephen R. Dodds	10th September 1943	62
1941	Burslem	H. E. D. Mabbott		
1942	Reading	R. P. Tomlinson	3rd June 1943	62
1943	Nottingham	F. W. Beetham	4th October 1946	
1944	Manchester	C. W. Tebbutt		
1945	Leeds	H. Ibberson		
1946	Lincoln	D. W. Reedman		
1947	York	P. Timperley		
1948	Birmingham	Charles F. Lamb		

INDEX